RECENT REVIEWS OF
I HEAR A SEED GROWING...

...A REAL TREASURE; POWERFUL AND GRIPPING, HARD
TO PUT DOWN. ON SEVERAL LEVELS, GATELEY COM-
BINES INTELLECT AND SPIRIT WITH ACTIVISM. ...SHE
PERHAPS CAN ACHIEVE THINGS OTHERS MERELY DIS-
CUSS.   **THE BLOOMSBURY REVIEW**

EDWINA GATELEY IS AN ESSENTIAL VOICE TO CHRIS-
TIAN FEMINISM. A MODERN DOROTHY DAY... SHE
WRITES WITH THE AUTHORITY WE ASSOCIATE WITH
WOMEN SUCH AS ELIZABETH FRY AND THE BOOTHS.
                    THE CHURCH TIMES

EDWINA GATELEY IS A POET, MYSTIC, THEOLOGIAN,
MISSIONARY... (SHE) STATES CLEARLY: THE VERY NA-
TURE OF OUR PATRIARCHAL SOCIETY PRODUCES PROS-
TITUTES–AND PIMPS. **NATIONAL CATHOLIC REPORTER**

IN SHARING HER FIVE-YEARS' JOURNAL ENTRIES,
GATELEY INTRODUCES STREET PEOPLE – MEN AND
WOMEN WHO HAVE THE SAME WANTS AND NEEDS THAT
ALL OF US HAVE, BUT NOT THE SAME HOPES AND
OPPORTUNITIES.... I HEAR A SEED GROWING NEEDS
TO BE READ.   *NGER*

I HEAR A SEED GROWING

GOD OF THE FOREST
GOD OF THE STREETS

Edwina Gateley

foreword by
Rosemary Radford Ruether

SOURCE BOOKS
Trabuco Canyon CA

ANTHONY CLARKE
Wheathampstead Herts.

L/C# 91-193000

ISBN   0-940147-07-6   (USA)

ISBN   0-85650-100-X   (UK)

Co-published by: Source Books
                        P.O. Box 794
                        Trabuco Canyon CA 92678

                        Anthony Clarke Books
                        16 Garden Court
                        Wheathampstead Herts. AL4 8RF

Printed and Bound in the USA By KNI Inc. Anaheim

DEDICATION

In memory of my dearest friend, Maria Gabriel, who walked many long journeys with me. Maria died of cancer in March 1990. May this book be a testimony to the courage and wisdom of a valiant woman, sister and soul-friend.

Also in memory of Dolores, Irene, Rene, Lori, Susan, Cupcake, Cricket and Carol, and the many other thousands of women who have suffered early and violent deaths on our city streets.

And also for Susie, Jeanette, Mezzie, Maria, Tee, Barbara, Kim, Olivia, Karen and Jamie, and all the courageous women of Genesis House who continue to struggle for new life and hope against so many odds.

May this book make a difference.

Contents

FOREWORD...vii

ACKNOWLEDGEMENTS...xii

INTRODUCTION...xiii

Part   I   THE HERMITAGE
                Reflections Written in Solitude.......................1

Part   II   THE RETREAT
                Discernment of God's Call.............................33

Part   III   THE STREETS
                Life on the Streets of Chicago......................61

Part   IV   TEDDY BEAR'S STORY............................91

Part   V   A PLACE TO CALL HOME......................161

Part   VI   A NEW CREATION.................................287

FOREWORD

Viewed on one level, this book is the story of five years in the life of Edwina Gateley, a British Catholic lay-missionary. She moves from a year of profound contemplation in a hermitage in the woods, where she tried to listen to the word of God for her life, to a decision to work with prostitutes in Chicago, and to the founding of this ministry and the development of Genesis House as its home.

Viewed on a more profound level, this book is about what used to be called "God, Man and the World". It draws us into a profound grappling with the human condition, especially from the perspective of those most abused by patriachal society. It also forces us to confront those who abuse them, and those who remain indifferent.

This book is about the Christian challenge to be in ministry, to open ourselves totally to God, and to be presences of the healing power of God to others, -especially the most broken of God's children.

Edwina Gateley brings us into vivid contact with the people of the streets of Chicago, the homeless who sleep in doorways and parks, and who crowd the floors of the shelters and the tables of soup-kitchens. We meet the prostitutes who walk the streets or who wait in the brothels for customers, the pimps who abuse them, the johns who come for their services. We glimpse some of these figures as they pass along the edges of Edwina's ministry, as she talks with them in bars, brothels and on street corners. Others become familiar friends by the end of the story.

There is the Madam of the brothel which Edwina visits, who curses the world, yet who slips twenty dollars to Edwina to help with her ministry, and arrives with her 'girls' to listen to Edwina preach a sermon in a suburban church. Religion often mixes incongruously with prostitution in this story. The Madam has pictures of the Sacred Heart on her wall, and flings eggs on the table on Ash Wednesday, still wearing the smudge of ashes on her forehead, and insists that all the prostitutes must 'fast'.

vii

There is   the ex-priest who mixes sexual fantasies with religion and demands that the girls kneel naked before him while he 'forgives' them.

By contrast, the prostitutes often relate to God in a touching and authentic way. They are sadly aware of their failures, yet confident that God loves them, and is indeed the only source of their strength in a world that despises them. We have glimpses of the Genesis House community at prayer, often gathering spontaneously in the basement chapel: nuns, priests, prostitutes, johns, pimps and wino derelicts, gathered together as God's people, -a sign of that banquet-table in God's Reign, where all divisions which separate people are overcome.

Behind the world of homelessness, substance-abuse and prostitution lies another world. This is a world which is accepted as socially respectable, but is in fact the source of the abuse and abandonment which has landed this collection of broken people on the streets. Almost all the prostitutes have been abused as children, sexually and psychologically. They were raped when children by fathers, step-fathers, uncles and grandfathers. They were beaten and unloved by mothers and fathers.

The women fled from abusive homes to the streets, where they moved into new abusive relationships with pimps. The pimps sell them, beat them and take their money, keeping the women tied to them by controlling their bodies and spirits. Sometimes they kill them.

Yet the women fail again and again to break with these violent and degrading relationships. Why? Has something been deeply imprinted from childhood, equating love with hurt? -"He loves me, even though he beats me, robs me and degrades me" is the sickening refrain that runs throughout this story.

The women are not the only casualties of abuse and violence. There is Gypsy, a derelict wino, whose father made him kneel on grains of rice for hours without moving, and whose grandfather made him an alchoholic at age three. There is Eskimo Joe who claims he has never recovered from having to kill in Vietnam. The johns have

ىeir stories of lovelessness, although they can arrive at the brothel in their three-piece suits and then return to their world of 'respectability'. It is the women, not the abusers, who are criminalized. Even the police arrive, sometimes in uniform, to use the services of the prostitutes whom they later arrest on the streets.

The central figure of Edwina's story is Teddy Bear / Dolores, a Mexican woman in her late twenties who as a child was locked in a room by her mother, until she fled to boarding-schools and thence to the streets. The writings from Dolores' journal fill much of this book, forming a contrapuntal voice to the poems and journal of Edwina. Dolores alternates between life and hope, determined to throw off her alchoholism, and despairing self-destruction. Again and again we see Dolores pull herself from the depths of self-abandonment, remaking the resolution to be sober, to make something of herself. Side by side with Edwina, she learns to recuperate in the hermitage in the woods, to rejoice in God's nature and to believe in herself. Side by side with Edwina, Dolores speaks with God, and sometimes God writes a letter back to Dolores. God is there for Dolores, endlessly offering her the grace to become whole, to throw off the power of death. Edwina is there along with God, endlessly offering the same grace of healing.

But neither God nor Edwina can force Dolores to "choose life." Dolores has to choose it for herself. She must come to believe in herself, and value herself enough to remain committed to her programs of healing, education and self-support. This she finally cannot do. We watch with horror as slowly she slips back into the power of death, and loses the will to try again to live. One has the sense that, when all is said and done, she cannot visualize herself as having a future, a life worth leading. She dies in a transient hotel on October 3rd (or perhaps October 2nd), 1985.

As Edwina gradually recognizes her inability to save Dolores, she also grows more in understanding what it means to be in ministry, -what it means to be a channel of God's healing power to others. Grace cannot be forced on people. Just as it is a free gift from God, so too, it has to be accepted freely.

However abused by others, in the end, the prostitutes and the substance-abusers must take responsibility for their own lives, must decide to love themselves enough to stop letting themselves be victimized. Ministry with these, the most broken of our society, often becomes a ministry of waiting, of endless patience, offering help again and again, but knowing that only the victims can make the transformation.

Through this profound growth into the meaning of ministry, we also experience a reshaping of the being and nature of God. Gone is the wrathful, judgemental God who supports the hypocrisy of society towards its victims, especially sexually-abused women. And gone is the God who infantilizes us, does everything for us, and makes us dependent on forces outside ourselves.

The God that emerges on these pages is more often named 'she' than 'he', -more mother than father. But more important than gender-image, is the quality of divine love and power. It is the love that is both unconditional and 'tough'. At times it demands that the victims take the consequences of their self-destructive acts, yet always is there for them when they are ready to change. This is a God whose power does not compete with our own best energies, but who enters into our best energies, to enable our fullness of life.

This is a God who suffers with her children, who waits for them to respond, and who often loses in this sad vigil. This book is, finally, about Edwina opening herself more and more to God, emptying out her own demands to be the all-competent savior of others, learning to become the channel of God's loving, empowering and suffering patience.

Although there are many small victories, this is not a success story. Dolores dies in a transient hotel after three years of struggle to heal herself, after three years of patient outpouring of love from Edwina and the community that grows around Genesis House. Yet it is not a story of defeat. Although Dolores loses her life, her many small victories become sufficient redemption.

The mystery of crucifixion, of death and resurrection, comes to the fore at the end of Dolores' life, at the end of all our lives. Dolores falls to the ground and dies, like the seed that perishes in order to become the kernel of new life that rises again. From this seed, a tiny flower has pushed its way through the hard, mean streets of Chicago. Somewhere in the Cosmos a new redemptive reality has made a beginning and can become the source of new blessings. We Hear A Seed Growing...

Rosemary Radford Ruether.
Chicago 1989.

ACKNOWLEDGEMENTS

This book has emerged not only from my own experiences, but also from the support and nurturing I have received throughout its writing from the Volunteer Missionary Movement (VMM) community in the United States.

In particular I would like to thank:

Depaul Genska, whose tireless commitment to reach out to women in prostitution first challenged me to do the same, and

Su Hood, who was the great provider and sustainer in all my times of need, offering me the space and the facilities to be able to write whilst working on the streets of Chicago, and

Maria Gabriel, who spent many, many days applying her critical mind and wisdom to editing and pruning my passionate out-pourings, and

Maureen Donnelly, who deciphered, typed and printed out this manuscript well into the early mornings, and

the women of Genesis House whose sharing, pain and courage helped birth this book.

INTRODUCTION

I was always curious about prostitutes. From an early age I sensed the disapproval and scorn with which society and church treated them. It was made clear that such women were to be avoided and viewed only with horror, from a distance. But as I grew older I began to reflect more deeply and to ask questions. I wondered why women prostituted themselves. I came to realise that my own experience as a woman and in particular, as a Catholic woman in a male controlled, authoritarian church, has not been, like it or not, without its prostituting moments. I became more aware of how all women are inevitably conditioned to sell themselves one way or another, whether it is for approval, acceptance, love, security or, indeed, money. The very nature of our patriarchal society produces prostitutes - and pimps.

It was a gut-longing to get to know myself more deeply and to try to connect with the God within me that led me to a hermitage in Yorkville, Illinois. For nine months I lived in the hermitage in the forest trying to get in touch with myself as a woman, trying to be still and to listen to the God within me. I came to experience that God cared deeply about all people - particularly the ones who were hurting. The nine months culminated in a 30-day retreat where my experience was thrown against the history of salvation that had formed my own spirituality. These thirty days brought into my awareness how the nine months of solitude and reflection had birthed in me, after a great deal of struggle and resistance, a clear call to reach out and to make connection with my sisters in prostitution.

This journal is the story of my response to that call. It is a story of struggle, pain, courage and growing self-awareness. Most of all it is a story about women - oppressed, abused and hurting. Sometimes they die because it is too painful to live. But sometimes they survive and witness to the Resurrection.

With each generation of survivors there will come, I believe, a new and enlightened consciousness that will eventually bring about a more caring, compassionate world, a New Jerusalem where there will be no more abusers and victims, no more prostitutes and pimps, but only sisters and brothers on God's holy mountain.

PART I: THE HERMITAGE

Yorkville, Illinois.

1st October, 1981.

THE CALL

I am preparing to move
into an old trailer
in the forest.
For some strange or wild reason
I don't fully understand,
I feel I must.
In my guts,
I am afraid
I do not want to have much time
to think, or even to pray
as I plan what to take and
what to eat.
For if I do,
I may stand and cry aloud -
No! I cannot go!
Is it that I fear the
Ultimate Encounter?
The solitude? The loneliness?
Is it that I fear
utter, uncompromising nakedness?
A strange force, from deep within
drives me and impells me
insistently whispering in my
very veins -
"Come."
A consciousness of call,
very gentle -
almost imperceptible.
I hear the shriek of the winds and
the bitterness of their touch;
I see the trees shedding their leaves,
leaving the branches
black and naked.
I smell the first harsh scent of winter

freezing over the gentle earth
and I shiver before its
creeping nakedness.
Yet I am being beckoned to be part
of its relentless violence,
called to stand alone before
its blast.
And, oh, the gentle heart
so deep within me
shudders...
and whispers - "Wait"....
wait for the tender touch of
Spring,
wait until the snow melts and
the ice breaks at the thrust
of the crocus...
Wait till the birds sing again and
the new grass grows.
Oh, wait - until the earth
is once again creator
mother of new life,
until she herself
invites and warms me
and welcomes my touch.
Yet, I know
oh, I know in my very guts,
that now is the time.
I must say yes,
for I need the violence of
those winds,
and I need the bitterness of
that cold,
and I need the nakedness of
that solitude,
to touch and to hear
the gentle God within me.
I do not fully understand
what I am doing,
nor why.

I only know
I must go with my
doubts and my pain.
For, however crazy this seems,
anything else would be
senseless betrayal
of my own
integrity and truth...
But I'm not
on my own.

6th October, 1981.

THE HERMITAGE

The trailer came today -
a huge cumbersome thing
that felled three trees
to find its way and claim
a home-land.
I felt shamed by all the trouble
and sweat I was causing.
(It took well over an hour)
But Brother Francis - so simple and
so honest
only said -
"It's for God also."
Later on in the day
I came alone to see
"the thing" - my hermitage -
rested - planted in
the clearing.
And as I walked around this trailer,
my new home,
I found myself swearing,
fighting, struggling -
"What am I doing?

Ah, fool, why am I here?
Can I do this?
Why? Why?"
Oh - I am afraid, and that
is the top and the bottom
of it all.
Beneath this fear,
these constant doubts,
the only thing that
holds me is an inexplicable, yet
firm conviction that,
a myriad years before me,
for some wild, deep,
and so true reason,
a power and force
far beyond my understanding,
saw and loved
my clumsy trailer.
And I, Edwina,
alone and wondering,
stand there before it,
only knowing
it was meant to be.

16th October, 1981.

The place is surely beautiful - space, land and forest. Autumn is almost over and the last leaves are falling. They cover the earth and the landscape, reflecting its darkness in shades of grey, black and brown. It is as if all that is gentle and warm and inviting is being stripped away, and what remains is harsh and barren, though it carries, still, a beauty of its own. Nature plays out before me what I fear will be my own experience in human terms. Something in me recoils from such nakedness, for I love warmth and richness...and yet, deep within me there is a certainty which, for all my fears, gently tells me that all is well and that this is how it should be.

In this environment with the changing seasons around me, I prepare to move into the trailer in the forest. Each day I go down there to paint, clean or dig. It is a slow business - a struggle against time and weather. I am anxious to finish and to close the door before winter and the cold sets in. It is getting late - the cold already goes before me and the nights fall fast. I wonder sometimes what it is all about. Am I fooling myself? If this is what I should do - it does not seem at all sensible! And yet there is still an urgency in me - very gentle and not at all disturbing - which keeps me stubbornly moving on. It is good and right for me to be here trying to fulfill what I feel called to do.

20th October, 1981.

As time goes on there are more obstacles and frustrations - well-meaning advisors express all sorts of fears against the plans I have - to put a wood stove in the trailer, to try to insulate one half, even to try to live there during the winter! Some friends understand and quietly help and support - others are aghast and suggest all sorts of alternatives. I begin to feel impatience and frustration at these people who reflect my own fears and doubts. I may not always understand the way ahead. I may experience doubts and fears, but I know in my guts when God calls and moves me. I pray, at this time of transition, that God will keep me firm in my resolve.

10th November, 1981.

Tonight is my first night here in the "hermitage" - better known as "the trailer" in the forest. It has been a beautiful evening. Some friends, including Su, have been with me. We shared a precious time - starting with prayer - for the first time in my tiny prayer space. The "hermitage" was blessed and my friends were with me. And I am so happy that so much love is given freely to me.

Now they have gone, and I am left alone this first night -feeling a little apprehensive - yet sure that God is here. It all makes sense in a way I do not yet understand. As night thickens I sit in this silent place and look around me in wonder at the new home I have prepared. It is small, just an elongated room with a bed in one corner and a simple table and chair facing towards the large window which looks out into the forest. Two oil lamps and a candle give the room an atmosphere of mystery. I have no books - just a copy of the Bible, some writing material and a battery-run radio, but the space is warm and cosy and rich in color. In another corner sits my heavy wood stove surrounded by logs and kindling. At the far end is a small kitchen with a modest supply of basic foodstuffs and two gas rings to cook on. There is no running water but two buckets stand full to the brim of water from the VMM house outside the forest. There is a deep sense of peace and tranquility in this lovely corner.

I can only pray,"Lord, stay with me, for I am here only in response to your call which I do not yet understand. Stay with me, and help me as I say 'Yes' and begin yet again in a new search and a new journey."

14th November, 1981.

So far it's been more like a girl scout camping experience than anything else. Survival is pre-eminent! I've worked hard getting used to the wood stove, learning to cook beans, digging a vegetable patch, collecting logs and kindling, fixing oil lamps, sorting out water, freezing in the morning, etc. etc. I have tried to pray four hours or so a day - but it's been hard going. I hardly dare to think of a whole year here. At this point prayer means either sitting in the tiny prayer corner still and aware, or wandering through the forest in appreciation of God's wondrous handiwork.

I feel as if I'm setting out on a long, new journey and I get that awful feeling that I've forgotten something! Or is it that I just linger, looking back? I really need God's grace and strength to see this through. God has never let me down yet....

16th November, 1981.

All I can record is a rather helpless feeling of bewilderment and boredom. I'm doing all the things I think I'm supposed to be doing. I know I must establish some kind of routine just to keep a balance. Intellectually, I have some understanding of this calling. After all, many men and women throughout the ages have been called to solitude. But it is so difficult to actually get down to living it. It is especially difficult when I don't feel emotionally moved or involved. Each act, each movement is an act of the will. I believe because I want to believe. I act, I move without inspiration, without feeling. I believe.

I have a feeling that something needs to break, and I have another, very awful, feeling that it will be me. God, be gentle - I'm already going through culture shock! I don't pray for consolations or grace - I pray that I'll be faithful and confident - but I'd be very grateful if God were to give me a little shove! Tomorrow, I'm going to fast and my heart sinks at the thought - I'm not a joyful disciplinarian! In fact, I think I'm a lousy hermit! All I do is protest!

"Spirit of Wisdom - come up to meet me. The novelty of a little trailer in the woods wears off fast. When there's nothing left, come up to meet me...."

18th November, 1981.

I'm spending much time working outside while the weather is so good and I need to get as much wood as possible under cover while it is dry. I am grateful there is so much to do. The nights are long and silent and full of the flickerings of oil lamps and candles. The wood stove gets too hot. The kitten I brought to the trailer with me, plays and scuttles around and I am also grateful for that bit of life and silliness. God remains silent, and I remain unmoved, like a rock. I keep at the routine, believing that someday there will be life and joy and I will find some enthusiasm in my journey to God.

SILENT GOD

Silent God,
empty, sound-less,
like the long, dark nights
without life,
I wait, gently hoping,
for your touch which says,
"I'm here".
But the void remains,
Unfilled.
Silent God,
Why do you hide your face
from me?
Why withold your breath
which kindles life?
Why, God, silent God,
do you watch your loved one,
alone and waiting
yet not reach out,
to only whisper:
"I am here"
Yet I will wait and
I will watch,
and in my mind's eye,
soaring deep from my soul,
I will see and
I will know -
You are here.

23rd November, 1981.

I cry with the psalmist - "Lord, do not hide your face from me." There
is no consolation - no affirmation - just being here. I manage well
enough but I fight the insidious temptation which says, "What are you
doing here?...You are wasting your gifts and talents...."

And God is silent.

Prayer is life-less and much of the time I doze off. I am mechanically, doing all I must - the simple round of collecting wood, lighting the fire, preparing beans, cleaning up and feeding the cat. I also do some reading from the Bible, sit silent before God and pray the Office. Outside, the snow begins to fall, the temperature drops. I feel eccentric and a little ridiculous. God is silent. And I too, wait in silence and pray that I will be steadfast.

I look forward, perhaps too eagerly, to Sundays which I spend up at the VMM house - having a shower and washing my hair (oh - it's a beautiful feeling to be fresh and clean!), catching up on all the news, eating a good meal and sharing Bread and Wine with the rest of the community, a perfect Eucharist - it is surely a day to be enjoyed! I wonder deep within myself about the disadvantages as well as the advantages of taking one day off a week from this hermitage lifestyle. I seem to spend the whole week looking forward to the end of it, and it is an effort to return to the trailer.

9th December, 1981.

It is so easy to think I am wasting my time. It is Advent - a time of waiting, but I have never waited to do God's will - I have always just followed. Sometimes though, it seems that I am not so much following as standing by the wayside looking around. Maybe it is important to look around to get my bearings. I must allow God the freedom to leave me a while in a bit of darkness or vagueness. I am too impatient, wanting to see - to be aware - to be in control. There is nothing to hold on to here. There is nothing, except the trivia of small routine. There is no goal or purpose! I have no target - no plan to work through.....it leaves me at a loss. It requires nothing less than a leap in faith expressed best in these words, "Lord, I believe, I know you are here. Stay with me."

I am anxious and looking around for signs. I must stop looking or I will miss them. I am accustomed to action and clear direction, and my first instinct, if there isn't clear direction, is to create one! How hard it is to BE! I must believe that this time of apparent "messing around" and "pottering about" is part of a process of becoming available and learning to wait on God. God is not gone - it is only that I can not find God's face awhile. I didn't know it was so hard to listen in a very deep silence. I want to interrupt it or to fill it with my own words and noises - that would be very comforting and reassuring.

16th December, 1981.

This is my last night in the hermitage this year. It has been six weeks. Many people ask me what it is like. That's very difficult to answer even for myself. Nothing comes to mind as particularly marked or significant. The days and nights pass one after the other in unchanging rhythm. I try to be attentive and faithful: to pray constantly (but rarely do), to quietly do all the little things that are required to survive, to go for long walks, loving God, sit in my little "chapel" saying nothing whilst being aware that I am loving; for why else would I be there? I know I will always love others and love being with them. Maybe one day they will not compete with God, rather, they will be a special gift of God to surprise and delight me. It is only by immersing myself in God that I will truly and deeply love other people and value them as God must do. Then people and God will be in harmony within me and I will glimpse a piece of the Kingdom.

7th January, 1982.

Well, this is the New Year, and I am back after Christmas and New Year celebrations. They were full of life and people and good things! Now, I'm alone again and I know that this year will be an important one.I feel so lonely. That is all. Just lonely.

8th January, 1982.

> Let me not look for signs and affirmations,
> let me not compare myself with others,
> thinking I should be this or that or

do this or that;
Let me not have hopes or expectations,
make demands or bargains,
Let me just be here,
just be here.
Even when I do not understand....

9th January, 1982.

Today it all seemed so much simpler and clearer after yesterday.
Perhaps I came to a cross-roads? I have been nearly two months here
and, if I'm honest, I am here somewhat reluctantly. I've found it very
difficult. Could it be because I have never put my heart totally into it?
I know I have spent a lot of time struggling - protesting - complaining -
feeling very bored. What do I expect God to do? Appear?

I must sit and wait
all the time
for nothing and
for everything
Just be here
only to wait
only to love
and in all of it -
not knowing.
Yes.
That is how
it must be.

16th January, 1982.

LET ME

Let me walk with you
even if I must walk alone,
and in the dark.

Let me hear your whisper
even when my noise and clatter resounds
through day and dusk.
Let me be praying
even when my whole being flees restless
from your presence.

Let me be faithful
even when, afraid and helpless
I want to go my way.
Oh Lord! please,
just let me learn
to be with you.

24th January, 1982

JESUS OF A THOUSAND FACES

Jesus,
oh yes,
I had many images.
I put them in my books,
hung them on my walls and
round my neck.
And often I gazed critically at
countless other images
displayed grandly in museums,
art galleries and the finest books.

Jesus of a thousand faces.
Jesus of a thousand ways.

I found him Saviour,
decked with a million stars
in St. Peter's, Rome.
In Westminster he was Redeemer
rising in triumph

high above the altar.
And in Washington I saw the Shepherd
leading flocks
where they would not go.

Jesus of a thousand faces,
Jesus of a thousand ways.

And as I grew and tried
to grasp this Jesus,
a new one emerged
for every occasion and
for every bursting or broken heart.

Jesus of a thousand faces,
Jesus of a thousand ways.

But then, one night,
when even the smallest star
refused its light,
and my world was cloaked
in a thick, grey void -
My Jesus of a thousand faces,
My Jesus of a thousand ways,
uttered a great and anguished sigh,
ripping asunder
my books and pictures
dissolving a myriad works of art
and crumbling
every long-loved image

Then,
in the awful silence which
settled on my devastation,
the breath of God swiftly came
and blew away -

My Jesus of a thousand faces,
My Jesus of a thousand ways.

> And the Cross,
> dark and etched
> against my grief,
> hung empty and desolate
> in the greying dawn.

27th January, 1982.

The painful feeling of loneliness just won't go. It pursues me. Waits for me in every still moment. Everywhere I turn I face loneliness, an acute awareness of being cut off, just on my own. I ask God to fill the spaces, to fill the loneliness. It is all quiet and still.

I panic, feeling that I am no longer of any consequence, no longer involved, no longer the one always referred to. I have no role to play or fulfill. I have become nothing, except myself. Myself seems not as interesting when apart from others. I soon get restless in my own company....

In spite of my restlessness, I believe this nothingness is the only way really and deeply to get to know myself. Alone there is no audience - just an empty place to stand on my own and become very (and often uncomfortably) aware of myself. But, how I long for company, for laughter, for things done with others! All I seem to be doing is to consciously allow my past to die whilst not creating any future.

"God, fill this empty space!"

28th January, 1982.

GOD'S DAY

> What do I do or manifest?
> There is nothing to claim or possess.
> I only absorb the idle hours
> passing in unproductive dallying.

And, like a dreamy lover, I
am aware of being caught in
a gentle mesh of love and self-giving,
so fragile,
it would break with a gesture of possession,
so strong, it carries, without force,
the long day from dawn to nightfall,
without pause or disturbance.
All enveloping,
like a mist that permeates and sweeps
into its folds
that which it would caress.
I am absorbed, half awake,
unresisting, grateful
to be so loved and held in
this silent, lazy day which belongs
to lovers.

1st February, 1982.

DO I LIVE?

Oh, the air is soaked
in a passionate love!
Eluding grasp or taste
vibrating in intensity.
And here I am,
so small and brave,
carried before God
on a bursting wave
of this great love.
Yes, here I am,
simple soul,
fleeing from a pleasant world of
Spring buds and dusky evenings,
into a mighty storm
of life

that erupts like
a hot volcano.
Unleashing burning love,
pouring itself unsparingly,
caressing and covering
the small and the brave.

Tell me,
Spring buds and dusky evenings -
Do I live?

15th February, 1982.

A Dream

I was serving potatoes to a line of people. It was a menial and messy task. There were lots of people around and I was under pressure to spoon out all that potato! Then a sophisticated woman appeared in a fine blue suit wearing a very expensive perfume. She looked aloof and a little disgusted and she whispered, "You shouldn't be doing dirty work like this.....come with me, I'll see to it that you get out of it..." I was tempted. But the dream faded and I was still holding the potato spoon!

26th February, 1982.

I used to pray for the gifts of preaching and prophecy and wisdom. Now I pray for compassion and humility....I used to be fired with a tremendous zeal and enthusiasm - like a fighter longing for the battle and desirous of action. Now I feel very small and inadequate, yet still willing, but for what, I do not know. I used to shout and cry aloud my passion and love for God. Now I have no words left. I used to experience God's intimate love and graces. Now I experience God's silence and absence.

I have discovered in myself a deepening love and a more sure desire to serve; I am as passionate as ever yet somehow more rooted and more still. The sea is as deep as ever, but as I touch the depths I know it as less turbulent.

My restlessness is passed. There is, instead, a deep voiceless yearning-born more of God than of me, dependent more on God than on me, leaning more towards God's glory than my own effort in service. I hope I am beginning to understand what ministry and following Jesus is all about - ultimately, little to do with me and a lot to do with God.

> "Teach me your ways,
> for they are not mine
> and I have not yet learned them."

27th February, 1982.

It is very hard to pray today. I am constantly distracted and dozing off. A long day!

9th March, 1982.

One of the most difficult feelings for me to cope with is uselessness. My friends are busy and doing much good work, and I am doing nothing.

This experience undermines my pride, my dignity, my sense of self-worth. I am doing nothing! It is a painful experience to feel that I cannot make a contribution to anyone. But I am aware that it is important for me to learn to experience what it is like to be/feel on the periphery and to be a non-contributor. It is a new experience for me.

17th March, 1982.

TO SEE A LITTLE

I used to pray:
God, teach me your ways.
Now I pray:
God, that I may see a little.

This is because I came to understand
that God is teaching me different ways
all the time -
but I don't see them.

There are miracles of God's works and
signs of God's ways all around me
and in me.
I have to learn to focus properly,
or, perhaps, to look in the right direction.
I only, really, have to see a little.

1st April, 1982.

Sometimes I feel like a spring being held down -
tensing to be released.
could it be that I'm supposed to go the opposite direction -
downwards and
inside,
instead of
upwards and
outside....?

Spring is here. Everything seems so idyllic - there is sun and warmth,
blue skies, the leaves are budding, the birds are going crazy with
song....but still, I am restless. I struggle in faith to remain inactive.

I sit by the stream in the forest. I sit in faith. I struggle in faith, to believe I am NOT idling my life away. I sit in faith, knowing that, sometime, something will come of this. I have nothing but faith to go by. I've cheated like crazy - taking every available opportunity to leave the hermitage - sometimes for days at a time. Oh, such a reluctant hermit! I hope God finds it funnier that I do. Well, I shall keep trying!

10th April, 1982.

THE CREATIVE POTENTIAL
OF THE DEAD END

I have come up against myself
a wall -
a blank -
nowhere to go -
unsure, lost -
bewildered.
Creativity is released
in any death situation,
when we believe in life,
when we are people of hope.
For people of hope
there is never any real death
for death has been conquered by Christ
and life has been exchanged for it.
I have faced death often
in many different ways
and everything has seemed so hopeless life-less.
At the moment of death I am called
to a faith response
that defies reason.
If only we had even a scrap
of resurrection faith,
there would be an abundance
of life and hope

We turn away too often
in despair
in hopelessness
in tiredness
in anger
in self pity
in defeat.
We turn away from the Dead-End
the tomb,
because we are blind.
We fail to see the light
waiting to be called forth
to resurrection.
Jesus saw his dead-end coming.
Everything he worked and preached for
was crumbling around him.
The whole thing
was in a shambles;
his followers scared and confused,
but he never turned back
even when he got to the dead-end -
he walked right into it in faith,
and he destroyed death
and dead-ends.

26th April, 1982.

I believe that I had a false notion of what I am here for. I placed
expectations which were unreal. It was I, not God, who had
expectations of solitude, isolation, fasting, asceticism. Perhaps, I had
to continue in my efforts ultimately to discover more about myself. I
had to be alone to do this, for when I am with others I want to be in the
center of activity, always turning, looking outwards. While I am with
others I do not have the same opportunity to face or know my real self.
God wants me to learn that I do not need to be a heroine or martyr. I
just need to learn my own needs and limitations. My hermit-image has
been smashed by my own self discovery, and I feel freer and more at
peace than I have for a long time. The hermitage is not an end in itself

but only the means by which I am called to be faithful at this particular time. I am not here to prove anything - only, to learn a little. I am planning to make a thirty-day directed-retreat in July. I feel the need for "centering". So much has happened that I need to sort it all out.

3rd May, 1982.

A Dream

There was a beautiful forest - the trees were splendid - thick with leaves and foliage. I loved the forest. I must have gone away because I found myself returning to the forest, only to find all the branches and the leaves of the trees had been cut off! There was nothing but a mass of tree stumps! I was enraged - devastated - crushed. There were a lot of people around but none of them seemed concerned about the trees - as if nothing had happened. Those who had actually cut them down were surprised and nonchalant at my anguish. I cried a lot.

Could it be that, perhaps, I am to witness some kind of death in something I love deeply?

5th May, 1982.

Only an empty soul can be filled.

6th May, 1982.

I observed a stone in the stream. It was quite large and covered in moss and lichen. The stream flowed vigorously all around it, sometimes washing water over it and always caressing the sides of the stone. I imagined this stone was my soul and the water was the Spirit constantly flowing, washing, caressing, cleansing. Even though there were times when the top of the stone dried because the stream ebbed, it was firmly lodged in the heart of the stream and never entirely left dry.

It did not matter, either, how much moss or soil had gathered in the crevices of the stone - the stream soaked all of it.

We are never left entirely alone by God. God - refreshing and free - always moving over, around and in us. Spirit God, carrying us back and forth, gently but with force and power, sometimes hardly perceptible, and always, always there. We are embraced by the Spirit. We are loved. We are free.

11th May, 1982.

I am surrounded by trees and rich green foliage. The birds are singing crazily, a dog barks in the distance and I hear the drone of a bee. It is warm and the breeze is soft. I hear God everywhere. Here God rests, and breathes peace and deep joy into all beings. Here God delights in creation - so fresh and pure. How distant death and desolation seems now. I remember boredom and the fears as something of the ancient past. Today God is everywhere.

PRESENT

I have not entirely gone.
Oh, no.
For see, there, in the corner,
the cushion on which I sit
to share your silence,
is yet warm.
And feel, there, on the
small plywood shelf,
the stub of the candle lately burned
to honor your presence,
is yet soft and wet.
And smell, in this tiny room,
how the perfume of the wild flowers
I picked with joy for you,
floats still delicate around

Oh, no.
I have not entirely gone,
I have not entirely gone.
For listen, very carefully,
and you will hear
my heart beat
in the silence I left you
as I ran,
free, wild spirit,
into your splendid forest
to sing my songs
of love.

14th May, 1982.

THE GRASSHOPPER

I caught a grasshopper
between the slats of my louvred window.
I had watched her,
only a few moments before
hopping, playing,
carefree as the sunlight
that caught the smooth lines
of her tapered body -
wood-like, brown and gold.
I smiled at her Spring freedom.
Then, distracted, I turned away -
just for a few moments.
And as I came back to the window
I idly turned the handle which
closed and snapped shut
my louvred window.
Too late,
the horror gripped me.
The grasshopper was caught
hanging helpless by its

long, delicate legs.
The large brown eyes
stunned in death's surprise.
I felt a great sadness,
a sense of enormous loss for
something so small, so fragile,
so free.
I was glad I had not heard
her silent scream.

17th May, 1982.

LAST SONG

I sat,
caressed by the coolness
of the early sun
and listened
to a solitary sound
that carried the night.

Loud and sharp
against the silence
rang the glorious notes
of a late, lone bird,
full throttled as she sang
her last splendid song,
leaving my small mind
entranced and awe-struck
as darkness fell and
stilled the listening forest.

28th May, 1982

If we do not know ourselves - how can we freely give ourselves to
others and to God? It is like giving someone a parcel all wrapped up,

saying, "Here you are, take it, I give it," but we do not know what is in the parcel. Most times we are afraid there is nothing much in it anyway. We pretend, perhaps, that the receiver will tell us what he/she found inside. God knows us, but that is not enough. The measure of self knowledge involved in our giving is also the measure of love and trust that we are able to share. God receives and loves us all the more for our self knowledge. When we don't know or understand ourselves our act of giving is clouded by ignorance and blindness. We are not free either to accept and receive the truth that is found in others. We build relationships which are not free nor loving because they are not based on truth and I have, therefore, a real responsibility to get to know myself - why and how I act, and how I can learn to grow, and become a whole and free person. I can only give that which I first know and claim as mine to give.

Anything else is cheating!

31st May, 1982.

WHY

I don't think I need
to prove my faith
and love any longer.
It's not going
to make any difference.
You know
I won't give up,
I'll hold on anyway,
so, why,
why, God
are you silently dallying
and playing games
with me?
Don't you trust me?
Why do you keep
testing me -

leaving me - fast glancing?
When will your point
be proven?
When will you
bombard me again
with joys and blessings
I once knew?
Oh, so long ago, it seems!
What's the hold-up?
Why the wait?
Please, dear God,
don't leave me
so sad, so lonely
before the
barricaded store
of a million
joyous blessings -
waiting
to burst forth upon me and
caress me
like a prodigal daughter.

9th June, 1982.

Why am I here?   What am I doing?   I still feel useless, empty,
idle...like a sham, a phoney....I do more dreaming and wandering than
praying....I have no concentration....no staying power.   Well, no
staying power, except to stay here!

PULL ME THROUGH

Pull me through, dear God -
just pull me through
once more,
because I'm stuck and
it's dark, dear God -
just give me

a little pull.
Because there is no space
down here
and I cannot see
the sky.
Just give me
a little pull, dear God -
only a little pull,
for I want to smell
the morning rain
and feel the cold,
free breeze.
Oh, give me a little pull,
dear God,
just a little pull.

10th June, 1982.

I cannot teach or tell people how to pray, or how to be real communicators or how to relate. I can only hint at my awareness of it. Prayer is a personal experience of God, unique to each individual, thus revealing the incredible richness and myriad aspects of God. All I can pass on to others is my experience of prayer as an unique "I-Thou" relationship. God is unique and I am unique. I can affirm people as they open to such experiences in the hope that each one will find her/his own unique way and path to an intimacy only two lovers alone can share.

11th June, 1982.

The initiative belongs to God.

I am available as a woman is available to her lover. She knows her lover is there, she knows her lover will always come to her, but she does not always know the time or place. She searches in love and trust and when she does not find, she waits. This waiting is not heroic or masochistic - it is a personal decision to claim love and not let it escape. If anything, the woman is obstinate and single-minded rather than pious or virtuous! Time for her is infinite. She waits, and in her waiting, she sees.

A friend of mine, Maria once said to me, "The rocks and the earth.....we call dead matter because we cannot think slowly enough to see them live." There is a lot of wisdom there.

22nd June, 1982.

I am beginning to understand a little. It has been a long and lonely journey. I waited, not always understanding. I realise that I was not distracted with all sorts of experiences or events. God left me to experience aloneness, because I was the event.

It is the gift of myself which I have been left with, but I, like most people, was conditioned to depend on external stimuli and events. To come to know and love me - that is task enough. My ministry at this point is me. It is not my business to worry about where I shall go, or what I shall do. I know my gaze has often been directed outside myself and I have been anxious as to what God has been preparing me for. Old habits die hard! God's grace is there for me, has been there all this time: Know myself, accept myself, love myself, empty myself. God can best use the empty vessel, the broken pot. Will I truly be able to say, "Here I am", and at last, know what it really means?

25th June, 1982.

God watches with great love as a father/mother watches a child, lost to all, except the chasing of a butterfly in the garden.

LIGHT

God - the beginning and the end -
much bigger than all our little fears,
concerns and preoccupations.

We have only to look up -
take our noses from off
our feet to see the light,
then it can drench everything else.
In light -
even our little fears, concerns and preoccupations
become bathed in truth as well.
They dissolve as they are embraced.
We are afraid of light -
it is too naked.
Most of us prefer the shadows.
There is more comfort there,
but a lot less honesty.

The order and wisdom in the universe makes me aware of the order within me, the inner harmony which leads me, through self knowledge and self acceptance. "He declares what is past and what will be, and uncovers the traces of hidden things." (Ecclesiasticus 42:19) The traces of hidden things lead to personal understanding and liberation, uncovering the hidden motivations and impulses which tyrannise and control us. We are created to be free and to live in harmony with all nature - nothing need be added or taken away. "How desirable are all his works...God has made nothing defective." (Ecclesiasticus 42:22,25) How much more must God long for harmony for humanity?

28th June, 1982

In a few days I start my retreat.

PART II: THE RETREAT

JESUIT RETREAT HOUSE - July, 1982.
(Barrington, Illinois)

Day One:

I AM TIRED

This is the beginning of my retreat.
I am tired and sad,
still trembling, still fragile,
knowing in my soul that
God is gentle.
But I am still a
little afraid that I might
crumble and die
if I hurt anymore.
All I can pray this evening is:
Mother God, Father God,
gather me up
in your arms - and
let me sleep....
I feel like a child
left alone in the dark too long.

Day Two:

"My name is John...I was on the island of Patmos for having preached God's word and witnessed for Jesus; it was the Lord's day and the Spirit possessed me, and I heard a voice behind me shouting like a trumphet, 'Write down all that you see in a book...'" (John 1:9-10)

John on Patmos. I remember years ago, sitting in a cave on the island of Patmos in Greece. According to tradition, John experienced there the visions which he recorded in the book of Revelations. I saw the rounded stone which served as his pillow, and wondered if he was feeling low and alone and afraid. The Lord appeared in a vision - "Do not be afraid", and instructed him to write down all he saw to the seven churches.

I am John. I feel as he must have done - abandoned, bewildered and a bit fed up. I am on an island - cut off, alienated. How can I understand all this? How can I make sense of my chaos? Who can call me to rise from desolation? I am imprisoned and suffering for preaching the Good News.

The vision that came to John came from behind him. I understand that - God does not come at us headlong - more like sneaks up on us, I think! Perhaps God will creep up behind me and shine a little light? Maybe my eyes will shine like a burning flame? Maybe my feet, refined in the furnace will be like burnished bronze? Maybe my voice, like John's, will be strong again and my face will shine like the sun? Maybe my words will be powerful as a double-edged sword? And I, who have "fallen in a dead faint", and have known desolation so long, will rise up from where I fell and write down all that I have seen.

Day Three:

"The lamp of God had not yet gone out, and Samuel was lying in the sanctuary of Yahweh...when Yahweh called, 'Samuel! Samuel!.' He answered, 'Here I am.' Then he ran to Eli and said, 'Here I am, since you called me.' Eli said, 'I did not call. Go back and lie down.' So he went and lay down. Once again Yahweh called..." (1 Samuel:3-6)

I am Samuel. I am lying in he sanctuary of the Lord - and the lamp has not yet gone out. There is still a little light left - just enough for me to recognise where I am, but not enough to see clearly. I am lying down because it is night and I am tired and very weary. It has been dark a long time. It is while I am sleeping in the dark that I hear God's voice calling me. I hear it. I get up to go outside and see, but there is nothing. I am disturbed. I sleep again, and again I am disturbed by the call - but there is nothing. I do not see my God - I no longer hear anything beyond that call which ended in silence. Each time I look outside, there is nothing. Darkness.

A third time I hear the call and I go again. Now I am distressed, bewildered. But I don't go away. I stay there in the sanctuary where the light of God is very dim but not yet out completely. I hear the voice again. I do not get up to look or see - I only remain here, for I am tired and I cannot see. I stay with myself. But I can still speak and I am still waiting:

"Speak, Yahweh, your servant is listening."

THE WAITING

God prepares me for his great grace
with a thousand blessings - unseen.
God tutors my soul with a constant caress,
elusive, warm, yet unfelt.
God unleashes on me a mighty tenderness
creeping around my inky night -
like a stranger not met,
Oh, God, prepares me for his great grace!
Gathering a myriad store of joys to fall upon
this wandering child of night.

Day Four:

"I was on that journey and nearly at Damascus when about midday a bright light from heaven suddenly shone round me. I fell to the ground and I heard a voice... I said, 'What am I to do Lord?' The Lord answered, 'Stand up and go into Damascus, and there you will be told what you have been appointed to do.'" (Acts 22:6-7,10-11)

I am Paul. I am on a long journey - it is my life. During my journey I am struck down blind and I cannot see. I am aware of a power/presence in my life but I cannot see. I am blind. God's light - raw - is too powerful for me.

In what ways am I persecuting the Lord? And what am I to do? I have been led here, to this retreat, in my confusion as Paul was led into Damascus. Here I will be told what I "have been appointed to do." I am having such a struggle. I went to Eucharist this morning and suffered through it. The language was sexist, the theology unsound - idealising suffering and presenting sacrifice as the means of loving.

No - the cross was a scandal. The myth of calling us all to sacrifice in order to love is not wholesome. It is a distortion. The feminine approach is creative - calling forth love and gentleness. I have endured too long the misguided theology of sin, and guilt, and sacrifice. It has oppressed me all my life - made me, so called, strong and brave! It has repressed in me a native tenderness and a natural longing for love without strings attached, a love which says, "Love me for who I am and not for what I have done for you." But oh, how alone I feel in all this. Sometimes I feel I do not belong here within this Church where I have so long experienced injustice and prejudice. It is as if I am trespassing and the terrain, though once familiar, is now strange and hostile. I am a stranger. I am afraid. Yet, this is my house, my church.

Dreams

I was kneeling by the altar with four priests at Eucharist, and I suddenly knew I was in the wrong place. I got up and walked out into the street. Someone was waiting for me. She said she had been waiting for a long time. She took me to an old house where there was a family in trouble. It seemed that the struggles of the world were separate from the church which concerned itself with rites and liturgies but not with the poor. I returned to the church and it seemed to be an old mansion. It was full of cobwebs and dust. I felt a great nostalgia and love for it, for once I was mistress of the house. Now it was filled with shadows and neglect.

These dreams, fit with my feelings of not belonging now. I am afraid - how could I leave my Church? It is here, in this womb that I was conceived. The Church bore me and gave me meaning in my life. Yet, how can I remain?

Oh, God, show me that all this is a delusion!

Day Five:

"Shepherds ought to feed their flock...you have failed to make weak sheep strong, or to care for the sick ones, or bandage the wounded ones." (Ezekiel 34:3-4)

Increasingly, I have experienced misused power and authoritarianism in the church I have always loved. I am more honest when I am able to acknowledge my pain at experiencing prejudice in the church. I am banned and oppressed as a woman. This church has smiled upon me, applauded me as a good, obedient girl. But now, I have become a woman. I have loved and served my church. But now she is like a pimp, oppressive and tyrannical. I do not think the church is being faithful The people are not being fed, nourished, comforted. We are feeding people with stones instead of bread. The Good News is freedom from all that binds us, socially, politically, economically or spiritually. Yes, it must have been a hell for Ezekiel to witness the blindness of his own people, his own tribe, his own family. I feel like Ezekiel!

I do not want to see my mother pimping - especially when she does not know it. But, in my passive obedience and acceptance of my church's power structures, am I prostituting myself? Am I contributing to my mother's pimping? The more I am aware of God's compassion the more I feel we are not a compassionate, caring church.

This morning is somehow, inexplicably, filled with peace. As I walk through the grounds I am very conscious of how beautiful life around me is - God is breathing everywhere. I reflect on how everything I value seems to have been cut down before me - the church I have loved and much of its traditions now leave me like a stranger without a home. Here I am, looking at mother church, for whom I am a child, but who neither nourishes nor wants me as a woman. She needs me but does not know it yet. She needs my brothers and sisters who have grown to be men and women, and continue to give birth to love and hope in our world, but she is too blind to see. I am sad and grieving, yet there is peace.

Day Six:

I sense a strong and all-prevailing spirit rising in me to replace this mother church I have lost. I have been touched by the image of God as Mother. This morning I prayed that Mother God will show her face to me. God has planned a future full of hope. God waits for my response - God is my mother, who gives the gift of life freely. But I must call, I must seek - then God will listen and I will find Her. Much of the action comes from me. God waits - like a mother waiting for her child to be born, while the new life turns in the womb. I am excited. I experience joy because I am being called to give birth. I am called to be creative as God is creative. I, who have received, must now bring forth new life.

I remember, last week, rescuing a baby chipmunk from the cats. I held the tiny thing in my hand - it was all wet and trembling - its mouth was open in fear and its eyes were wide and beautiful. It was shivering. I remember the great sweep of compassion I felt for the struggling thing - how large and powerful I experienced myself over and against the frightened baby chipmunk. I wanted to show a kind face to it. I wanted to protect it, console it, but it was so afraid it tried to bite me. I wanted the little chipmunk to understand that I was loving it, protecting it - even in its fear.

I have thought of it often since then. I feel like the chipmunk. Maybe that is how God experiences me as she holds me in the palm of her hand. Her love is far deeper than I could have felt as I held the chipmunk. I am in her hands - longing to allow her to love me - but still kicking and biting.

I did not let go of the chipmunk until it was safe. I know, and now feel, that God will not let go of me until I am safe. I am far, far more precious in God's eyes, and yet, how I loved that chipmunk! How God must love me!

GOD IS

God is the water in which I swim
she is the air which I breathe,
she is the life around me.
She is all and none of this.
But, close to me, she is.
I have sung and I have danced
whenever I felt her touch.
I have jumped and played,
but when I felt that she had gone,
I sobbed like a grieving child.
I remember the forest - the heights and depths,
the light and the dark,
the desolation and the consolation.
And all the time God was there -
the darkness was only dark to me.
She did not hide from me.
I was blind to her weaving a delicate and
beautiful plan of salvation
within my very darkness.
The wonder of ourselves!
The wonder of myself!
Yes - I feel the fragility,
of myself.
I am the new creation, created, creator.
I am the Spring waiting to burst,
while my God gently,
gently calls me forth -
to the wonder of Herself!
I am.
God is.

Day Seven:

"When Israel was a child I loved him, and I called my son out of Egypt. But the more I called, the further they went away from me...." (Hosea 11:1-2)

I cry for God's pain; I cry for the children.

I experience the vast loneliness of motherhood. I am torn by the anguish of the God Mother, unable to part from that to which she gave birth, until her creation is free. I tremble. I am both Mother and Child. I see God tremble! I cry for the God who is real enough to tremble. If we knew how God loves us, we would tremble and cry, but we would not be afraid anymore. So often we are blind but we do not know it. Many times we are silly - like sheep who have been led astray. We don't really want to be lost. God understands that. The tragedy is not the anguish of God but the blindness and the fear of God's people.

I cry for the people too! I cannot rest with a joyous faith unless my faith also calls others to freedom and joy. Personal faith only makes sense when it is in relation to others - it cannot contain itself. It overflows and it cries.

Day Eight:

"God saw all that God had made, and indeed it was very good."(Genesis 1:31)

I feel like an integral part of the whole of creation....I want to love and care for it because everything created is for my good and my joy. I stop to talk to the birds and the flowers. I fly with the butterflies, awed by the night, refreshed by the morning. I delight in the garden God has put before me. I see a beautiful bunch of lilies. They are splendid, growing in the garden. But they are too tall for their weight and they bow at an angle. I lift them up and say, "You're beautiful! Don't hide! Show yourselves, and make this place an altar to our God." Everything I see praises God just where it is, and I walk and run by it all - enjoying it all. This is my prayer, my hymn to God. This is my participation in creation - loving it, calling it to fulfillment to be the delight of humanity.

Day Nine:

"He was not the light, he was to bear witness to the light." (John 1:8)

I feel secure and safe and small. Someone just gave me a lamp and it is warm to the touch. The light shines for me and for others. I hear myself saying, "Hold it up and they will see." As I hold the lamp up, the light is above me, so I myself do not see it, but I feel it and my hold is very strong. I am happy to hold the lamp up. It is what I should be doing.

Day Ten:

"How lovely, all God's works, how dazzling to the eye!" (Sirach 42: 22)

There is such harmony and beauty in nature and, indeed, in the universe given to us to care for. How much more should there be in the greatest of God's creation - us! I learn from even the smallest creature around me, that I, too, am called to be a creation of grace and wisdom. God has made nothing defective. All is created for glory and beauty....

I only need to look out to the world to see God's truth, and when it is dark outside, I only need to search inwards, for truth is also within me. Only a few people believe themselves beautiful. That saddens me: it is a diminishment of the human potential for grace and excellence. I would like to help people believe in their infinite potential for beauty - otherwise when we all diminish ourselves, we diminish God also. I want to call forth the seeds of beauty that God has planted in such abundance.

Day Eleven:

"As he is the Beginning, he was first to be born from the dead, so that he should be first in every way; because God wanted all perfection to be found in him and all things to be reconciled through him and for him, everything in heaven and everything on earth, when he made peace by his death on the cross." (Col.1:18-20)

I have to rise from all my own little deaths so that I might be a channel of peace and reconciliation. Jesus was the first to rise from the dead. His tears, his blood and his sweat became a symbol of hope for the world. His life was a sign that God calls us to fullness. But I do not have to wait for a physical death. I am called to rise all the time from death imposed by myself and others -

<blockquote>
the death of trust
the death of harmony
the death of kindness
the death of forgiveness
the death of love....
</blockquote>

All wholeness emerges, rising from all deaths. We do not have to die on a cross. I die when I am unfaithful to my relationship with God, nature and other human beings. I resurrect when I allow trust, harmony, kindness, forgiveness and love to become a healing force in my relationships - when I give or receive, in love. Resurrection is breathing upon me all the time. God is always enticing me to justice and faithfulness. The challenge and wonder of resurrection is before me almost every moment. Resurrection is a daily event.

Day Twelve:

Dream

I saw a place I knew in England - a place famous for its stone and its wild, barren landscape. I saw huge piles of stones scattered everywhere, and walls made of stone stretched for miles. It was very clear, but I did not understand.

God said they were like people whose hearts had become like stone. God was angry. I understood that God was angry at our violence - our deliberate death-planning in nuclear arms and the death-planning of our planet. Then, as I began to despair, I felt the image of the Mother God rising. She said she wished to unleash torrents of water from the womb of her creation, to wash over the harshness, the dryness and roughness of the stones. The Word is always forming in earth's womb. It is constantly brought to birth in darkness.

Day Thirteen:

I had a vision of a great stone - it was blocking the tomb where Christ lay dead. I was to move the stone so what was in the dark could come into the light. I knew I would have to creep into the tomb before I could remove the stone. It could not be pulled from the outside but only pushed from the inside. It would be very dark in there, but I knew I must enter.

I cannot meet the darkness of others until I have met my own darkness.

THE LILY

I am the lily, bowed and bruised
even in my beauty.
God came and plucked me,
fed me with water though I was dying,
and carried me with a thousand kisses
into the bosom of my Mother's House.

Day Fourteen:

"...as the clay is in the potter's hand, so you are in mine, House of Israel." (Jeremiah 18:7)

I am clay in God's hands and at times I may or may not be supple, or not responsive to God's gentle shaping. Many different things can be made from the same batch of clay - I was a teacher - an administrator - a preacher - a student - a hermit - a lover. I have been many things - I have been formed and called into different ministries - but it is the same Edwina.

As long as I respond - God can continue to shape my own individual path in me. God is forever introducing me to new and exciting challenges. God only asks that I respond. I need to be flexible and open to the new creation and the new call that is forming within me. God can form a huge pitcher out of me and fill it with water to pour on the dry stones. I must wait to be renewed and reshaped. The more clay is worked, the more pliable it becomes in the experienced hands of the potter. I must remember that I, too, am called to be potter, creator of love. I feel a deep peace and a sense of something being created - or being brought to birth. Perhaps the Mother God will show me her face and show me how the clay becomes the potter.

Day Fifteen:

"Yahweh said to Moses, 'This people...will desert me and break this covenant of mine that I have made with them.'" (Deut.31:16)

"Now write down this song which you must use; teach it to the sons of Israel, put it into their mouths that it may be a witness on my behalf against the sons of Israel." (Deut.31:19-20)

God told Moses the people would be unfaithful. God tells me we are unfaithful people. In giving Moses a song for the people to sing about their unfaithfulness, God is reminding them of the Covenant. It is not so much a condemnation as a call to healing. God only turns away when angered and frustrated by our stubborness. However, God always turns back, choosing healing and reconciliation. Or why would God bother giving the people a song to learn at all? God wants us to recognise our unfaithfulness and opt for healing. God has given me a song. I, too, have a song to sing. My song calls people back to God as Lover. My song invites them to see the compassionate face of a

Mother God. I sing of the Passionate God. We are often blind and silly. Our images of God are so limited. God is very patient. Passionate God. My song is a birthing song, the birthing of the compassionate woman in me. The face of God will not be revealed to me until it is revealed in me. This involves active participation in my own birthing process.

Day Sixteen:

"See the days are coming - it is Yahweh who speaks - when I will make a new covenant with the House of Israel.." (Jeremiah 31:31)

The new covenant which God makes is to be written deep within my heart. This covenant must be slowly sunk in to reach its depths, and must be continually called forth from the deep recesses of my being. It is a searching, probing process into all which binds and oppresses me. It is a painful process and requires the nurturing of myself with time and care.

I can't expect instant conversion like instant coffee!

Day Seventeen:

"Feed my sheep." (John 21:17)

I have heard that before - many times in prayer. I hear it now very clearly. I followed Christ as King, I was the soldier, the fighter. Now I see Christ as Shepherd, shedding the image of Christ as King. "Feed my sheep." Who will feed the sheep?

It is the compassionate woman who will feed the sheep - not the soldier in you. You have fought a good fight. Give birth to the compassionate woman. I am aware of the struggle. I am leader, guide, catalyst. But the compassionate woman follows, tends, feeds. I am afraid of changing roles. Where is the King? The battlefield? Where are the soldiers? I am a good leader, but I only see the Shepherd and all he says is - "Feed my sheep."

I want to fight. Can I feed? I am trained to fight and struggle. "Feed my sheep." I turn away - I feel very sad - I am still afraid. "Feed my sheep." Why am I afraid? I have been a soldier for such a long time. But is it the compassionate woman who will feed the sheep. From soldier, strong, unyielding, to woman, life giver, nurturer.

Day Eighteen:

"In the sixth month the angel Gabriel was sent by God to a town in Galilee called Nazareth, to a virgin betrothed to a man named Joseph, of the House of David; and the virgin's name was Mary." (Luke 1: 26-28) Mary was afraid. She questioned and doubted. In the deepest recess of her heart she knew, with a great faith, what God was doing, but she experienced many times of darkness. She had many moments of doubt, but she never said No to what God called her to be, the mother. She held on against all the odds. Faith manifested in darkness. The greatness in Mary does not lie in a passive, shining light of instant and frozen submission, but in her simple and profound faith which said Yes to that which she did not fully understand or comprehend. She said Yes to that which, even in the end, culminated in apparent failure and death. Her greatness is in her faith, strong and profound.

Mary's giving birth to the Word was a messy process, conceived in darkness, brought forth into darkness. She had to feed, clothe and wash Jesus. Could this helpless infant be the Word of God? Mary had to nurture the Word. He was dependent on her for food and sustenance. She fed the Word in darkness. She was a compassionate mother. She responded not because she understood but because she believed.

Day Nineteen:

FLIGHT

I scrambled down the stairway -
ran out into the open air,
escaping the Wisdom born before the sun.
I hid beneath the thick leafed trees -
stilling their rustle of betrayal.
I chose the path barely trod
where I would meet no other,
and wished the warm black earth
would draw me into its darkened bosom.
I dodged the sun
chasing me
as dancing light between the leaves.
I stopped my ears
that in the awful silence
I would not hear God's thunder.
I crept, tiptoed,
so God would not hear
the heartbeat of my step.
But everything I touched
turned to God and looked at me -
stunning my flight -
awed at my betrayal.
Running, stumbling
through creation
I fled Creator.
Weary at last
I stopped,
but even in the very breath
I drew in my dying,
breathed the Living Creator
whom I fled.

Day Twenty:

"While they were there, the time came for her to have her child, and she gave birth to a son, her first-born." (Luke 2:6-7)

I am with Mary. It is uncomfortable, the floor is hard, the straw harsh. It is dark. Mary is afraid. She is praying. Mary is in pain. She is giving birth and it is painful. She is crying. Joseph is concerned. Worried. It is hard to breathe. The air smells of cow dung. Mary gasps and cries. The child is born. Mess. Smell. Dark. Pain. This is the birth. It is painful and dark. Mary fell asleep from exhaustion soon afterwards. She prayed in thanksgiving.

I too, must give birth - give birth once again, to the Word in darkness. That is how the Word was born and that is how the Word will always be born. I have to believe in the obscure and awesome wisdom of a God who was born in the cow dung. I have to understand what that means for me, the divinity in the dung, the mystery in the mire.

"Give birth! Go to the stable!" I must start again, naked with only God. Go back to the stable. "Don't be afraid. Give birth again!" I must start again with nothing.

I feel more peace than I have done all day. I can smell flowers!

Day Twenty One:

"It was at this time that Jesus came from Nazareth in Galilee and was baptised in the Jordan by John." (Mark 1:9)

Jesus came freely to be baptised and he chose a man, John, with whom there were ties of friendship, family and love, thus affirming the "human" aspect of his mission. He accepted a world where relationships were broken, where oppression and injustice were accepted and practiced by the political and religious leaders. Through his baptism he acknowledged that he was part of this world - and he prayed - and the Spirit of God came upon him. The Spirit of God will also come upon me when I accept and embrace the condition of my world. I will then take part in the redemption of the whole of creation. I will then be involved in God's saving plan.

The compassionate woman bows to truth and in accepting the reality of her self, also accepts the reality of the pain, suffering and sin of the world. The compassionate woman is one who sees her people hurting and gently grieves. She does not stand heroic and brave before the reality. In her love she grieves, in her compassion she reaches out even to that which causes pain. I must go to my Father's house, to my Mother's home. I experience a deep peace here in this sacred place, a belonging. This is my Father's house, my Mother's home. I must not leave it. This is where I belong. I was born to be in my Father's house, in my Mother's home. God's way is that I, as mistress in my Mother's home, must immerse myself in human chaos. In this chaos I will find order and truth. Will I submerge myself in human chaos - in the pain of people who are hurting and considered inconsequential? Will I walk into that kind of darkness with the homeless, the poor, the marginalized? What about the prostitutes? Who cares about the prostitutes? Will I walk about with the prostitutes? Is that what I must do?

Day Twenty Two:

"Filled with the Holy Spirit, Jesus left the Jordan and was led by the Spirit through the wilderness, being tempted there by the devil for forty days." (Luke 4:1-2)

Temptations...This is ridiculous, I am just fantasising. Be steadfast, Mother God, sustain me in this desert. My head is filled with strange, sharp voices, "Use your gifts - don't waste them, don't hide them in the earth." (But where is the pearl of great price?) What a waste. Talented. Gifted. Speaker. Writer... You can make an impact... You inspire people... You can hold an audience... You could do a lot... Would you be a worm, burying yourself in the earth? The people need a revolution... There is too much oppression and corruption in the Church... There are good people waiting for you! The prostitutes can take care of themselves... The Church is more important... Be reasonable, be sensible... Don't get carried away with silly ideas about prostitutes... It's just a novelty... Your very temptation is this silly idea!

You're just trying to be different... You're just getting hung up on this silly romantic notion of bringing light into darkness and feeding the lost sheep - who don't want to be fed anyway. They don't want you. God doesn't depend on you for their salvation... They'll never care for you... Leave them alone! You need to think of all the gifts that God has given you and the good you could do. You know you have a lot of charism... Don't throw away all that has been given to you! Remember you're an intelligent, sensible woman... You come from a very solid down-to-earth people... Cut the crap, the dreams and the visions, and go home, do a good job and enjoy it! Your temptation is always to go for the toughest, the hardest road... When will you learn that is not what God wants - that's pride!

Voices - voices - voices....strange sharp voices. Seductive...sharp.

I need a break!

Day Twenty Three:

Reflections at Eucharist.

Stay in my Father's house. This is my Church, my home.

I look around at my church and its leaders, conscious still of an alienation - a woundedness. I realise I am to love them, the leaders, even as I wince at the oppression and injustice they perpetrate. I have to stay with it. That is what my baptism is for. Immersion in all of it.

I sit and celebrate the Eucharist with all men at the altar - knowing it to be unjust. The Compassionate Women are excluded from the altar because we are told we don't image Father God. They do not know the Compassionate Mother God who always includes all her children, who feeds and nurtures them. I do not accept this oppression, but rather I immerse myself in the very mess of it. How easy it is to deceive ourselves when we hold on to the image of a Warrior God King. This image validates the inequality and the wrongful use of power to maintain a hierarchy. How far away from the Sheep the Shepherds get when they gather to celebrate with each other. They set themselves apart, even convince the Sheep that this is the order of God and the Universe. But the Mother, Compassionate, Nurturing God does not validate anything but to love one another

Day Twenty Four:

"Then, taking him aside, Peter started to remonstrate with him. 'Heaven preserve you, Lord,' he said, 'this must not happen to you.'" (Matthew 16:22-23)

It was the cross that Peter would prevent Jesus from standing under. The cross is the sign of contradiction. I could avoid it quite rationally and plausibly. I can! There are so many good things I can do, without all that dirt and darkness. But I will not do what I want to, but what I have to. I will be taken where I rather not go.

"Feed my sheep." The bread of life is not to be consumed like some private piety - it is to be shared and distributed for the nourishment of many. I want to be involved in that sharing and distribution.

"Feed my sheep." My "temptation" is all about life and being life-giving. It is not about bringing light to the darkness, but simply living in the darkness.

Day Twenty Five:

Today I had a vision: There was a woman - old and gentle. We embraced but did not speak, only looked, and in her eyes everything was said. Here, in the unspoken words, in the love and longings of her eyes, in the gentleness of the gestures, in the very tenderness and depth of her being - here was my Compassionate Woman. We sat on the floor in the corner. We drank hot, sweet tea. Never spoke, but gazed upon each other for a long time. She called me Woman. I called her Mary. Old. Gentle. The Compassionate Woman. She leant over to me, embraced me, and then held my hand - I felt hers rough. She was crying - there were tears running down her face. She was suddenly sad. "Be compassionate. Don't condemn. Love."

Day Twenty Six:

"The cohort and its captain and the Jewish guards seized Jesus   and bound him." (John 18:12)

I saw Jesus bound
and a thought flashed into my mind:
Prostitutes are bound.
"Go to those who are bound."
Increasingly, I am seized with a great grace,
taken by surprise.
Grace upon grace.
All I see is Jesus bound.
"Go to those who are bound."
What shall I do?
"Unbind them!"
In my night there is a moon,
which illumines, to lesser or
greater degrees my life.
In the lives of those who are bound,
there is not even a tiny star.
"Unbind them!"
The dignity of Mary.
The dignity of women.

Day Twenty Seven:

AFTER THE CRUCIFIXION

I

The Compassionate women
sat together
gently rocking
in tear-less grief.
Tea,
frail and sad attempt
at consolation,
stood before them
in earthern pots
to soothe a thirst -
unsoothable.
Eyes, half-veiled,
filtered through
the soul's deep horror.
Outside the house
little knots of
numbed followers
stood and crouched -
dumbfounded.
The very air,
breathed from
human despair,
was motionless and still.
Hush, Mary, hush.
Give me your hand.
Rest gently
on my breast
and the bitter horror
of cruel death
will be soothed
at the steady, strong beat
of my heart.

Hush, Mary, hush.
A mighty compassion
consoles the Woman.
Hush, Mary, hush.
And the tea,
brewed hot and sweet,
waiting
to be drunk,
grew cold and tasteless
before the silent wonder
of pure and naked
compassion.

II

The day passed heavily
and sank
into dusk.
And then, oh, then,
a fear
crept upon me in the
stealth of the shadows.
I saw the splendor
of the Universe,
that sparkle of the grass,
and the proud majesty
of conifers and oaks -
rich foliage all around.
I saw the vast arch
of a darkening sky,
and heard a splendid
chorus of birds
herald life.
And for me,
I saw it all sink
beneath the dusk,
and all
that glorious beauty
was gulped into

thick darkness,
and the song of
the birds and the crickets
suffocated in a
heavy smoke.
I cried aloud -
Ah, no!
Do not steal
my day
and cast
my glorious universe
into death!

And then I heard
a gentle whisper
brush against
my cheek.
Hush, woman, hush.
Give me your hand,
rest gently
on my breast,
and the night
you fear
will be as day
in the shelter of
my love.
Hush, woman, hush.
Take my hand
and the pain of
the darkness
will be soothed
in the steady, strong beat
of my heart.
Hush, woman, hush,
for you will come out
of the living tomb
to the heart of my Son.
I shall carry you.

Oh!

You shall come
and you shall smell
the flowers.
The Compassionate women
sat together.
Gently rocking.

Day Twenty-Eight:

"He has risen from the dead and now he is going before you to Galilee;
it is there you will see him." (Matthew 28:7)

Christ is going ahead of me. The Advocate will come and the Spirit of
God will overshadow me.

Day Twenty Nine:

"Later on, Jesus showed himself again to the disciples. It was by the
Sea of Tiberias..." (John 21:1)

How often I fail to see the abundant gifts and graces freely given to me
by God - I think I labor alone and without fruit, much like the apostles
out fishing all night, catching no fish. I now recognise with greater
clarity what God has done in my life and I am amazed at the
abundance. God, in great love and concern prepares what I need
before I realise it myself. And God invites me with a word, "Come!" I
need God's nourishment to follow... In the face of all this grace I am
asked to declare my love for God - the call is clear and very personal:

"Do you love me?" It is important that I do proclaim my love.

I will not teach, preach, explain or guide, but simply witness to the
Spirit of Truth which is in me. The Compassionate Mother will be the
only truth and witness that I am called to present. As She lives in me
so all my life and being is in Her and all strength and grace is drawn

from Her, from Her secret places of great light and beauty. And the gift of this new understanding cannot be measured or explained. It can only be seen by the soul in a mysterious way. I cannot grasp or hold it, but only experience it. I offer my understanding to all and they will accept it in the measure to which they can experience and see. I know this understanding is a source of light and strength which, though occasionally may be hidden from me, will never come to an end. It can never be taken away. If I treasure this new wisdom, Sophia, the Spirit of Wisdom will transform me in all I am and all I do.

From the gutters and the dark back streets, from the squalor, human despair and misery will be created a new heaven and a new earth. Yes, it is already being done in those who believe and who are re-created. It is being done in me. The new Jerusalem, even now, rises up - hope against hope, defying the impossible with the gentle breath of the Spirit of God. And all those who weep and mourn and cry out in the darkness will see new creation and will say, "God lives in us."

"Go to those, my loved ones, my lost ones, my rejected ones. The ones who live by darkness. Go to those my people for whom I came, for whom I lived, and for whom I died. Invite them to the banquet. My Spirit will rise powerfully in the poor. There will be a new creation."

The oyster shell is rough and harsh and unattractive. At its heart, deeply hidden and waiting to be revealed, I will find the pearl of great price. The compassionate woman always knows it is there.

Day Thirty:

The compassionate woman is born, and there is a new harvest.

PART III: THE STREETS

19th October, 1982: Yorkville.

I am going to work with women in prostitution. I am not sure where to find them. First I must get to know the streets - wander around wherever I feel drawn. Only God could have got me into this! When I look around the streets of Chicago the whole thing just seems beyond me - so enormous. God is going to stretch me further than ever. I don't know anything about this business. I have no idea of what I am doing or what I am getting into. Ignorance is often braver and more willing than knowledge. Perhaps I should throw myself in on trust and faith alone, rather than try to equip myself with fore-knowledge. I am badly tempted. I dream of things I prefer to do - go home to England - get back into overseas mission - preach or teach. I feel very much alone... How much easier it must be to be told what to do, to be under authority and obedience, instead of having to take great leaps of faith alone. but I don't want to stop taking these leaps! "Please Lord - affirm me, don't let me weaken as soon as the first misgivings appear."

27th October, 1982: Yorkville.

I have no models - nothing which makes me say, "This is it", or "That is it". I can't go into this work with a plan of action. I can only go into it with a faith which says it is God's business and God will see to it. I have never felt so helpless and vulnerable before a task - I have to go empty- handed, and with a feeling of being one of St. Paul's "fools for Christ's sake". I still occasionally glance back to the past, where I knew what I was about, with nostalgia. I am aware of a fleeting sense of regret, and I feel tempted to believe I made a mistake, - "This is not where my talents lie. I don't belong in this dark path ahead of me!" Is it, perhaps, that I see an empty space for God to create and I am afraid?

11th. November, 1982: Washington, D.C.

When people ask me, "Why do you want to do this, what is your purpose?" all I can reply is that God wants me to do it. I never planned going into the streets, worked out how I was to talk to the women, analysed the statistics or researches made. All I have done is fight this idea! The idea of having any kind of a "plan" seems, in the circumstances, quite unnecessary. There are no models I can make use of. There is, however, a loud cry, screaming a need, and God hears the cries of her people and sees their suffering. All I can do is hear the cry too. That is plenty to deal with for the time being. It is best for me to get on with being in this place. When I try to plan, it all becomes confusion. God wants me to let the Spirit create and build. I have no control, but I still want to have it.

I am trying to make some contacts - meet people who have had some street experience. I have come to Washington D.C. where I visit Joe, who is gay and very outspoken for gay rights in the church as well as society. There is no place for him in our official Church, and less for women who are in prostitution. It is a pity that the Church has steeped herself in a narrow and exclusive morality for so many centuries. How long will it take for us to embrace those who are different? We are too arrogant in our righteousness! But those we have oppressed and marginalized are going to get up.....

It is good to have a sense for what is going on on the periphery of Church and society, if I am going to ever understand what this ministry is about. Well, I suppose I have always been on the periphery myself, so I should feel quite at home here. It is important to be aware of how people are "unacceptable" and rejected. Perhaps it is those who consider themselves the norm, who are in fact the periphery as far as God is concerned? Surely, it is more a matter of whom God may reject rather than whom the world rejects? What if we turned it all upside down and were able to see with God's eyes - the rejected and the oppressed are ourselves in our lack of charity and our prejudice? So, I ask myself, "Who is on the periphery? What is the treasure? Where is the pearl? Who are the chosen people?"

Tonight Joe took me around Washington D.C. We cruised around where female prostitutes stood in twos and threes on street corners. I felt so sad for them - waiting for hours in the cold to be used and abused. I wished I could reach them, touch them, talk to them, be somehow with them... I saw dozens of male prostitutes doing the same thing. We went to a bar where there were male strippers and hustlers. I feel depressed. I suddenly see my world filled with violence and human diminishment. This evening leaves me a bit numb. I am in this safe house, in a warm bed, and I think of all those prostitutes stamping their feet on the cold street corners waiting, hopefully, for someone to stop and pick them up. Why do they do it?

17th November, 1982: Yorkville.

Although I do not see how this ministry will actually work out in practice, I am quietly and gently assured of God's presence and grace. I try to live out the Gospel witnessing to God's works, "Do not worry what you shall say...." I must worry about nothing, nor try to plan anything. I must believe and love. The streets will teach me. The women themselves will bring God's ministry to flower. After all, it is theirs. I am only a catalyst.

GENTLE GOD

God is breathing gently,
God never hurries,
Is never anxious or pressing,
God just waits,
Breathing gently upon us
With great tenderness
Until we look to God -
And, knowingly,
Nod.

22nd November, 1982: Hermitage, Yorkville.

I am grateful to still have my little hermitage in the forest to come back to for rest and prayer and to keep my perspective. I walked in the forest at dusk and wondered at all the blessings I have been given. I have fallen in love with this forest - it whispers God's name everywhere. I look at my hermitage and remember last year....the months I spent living in this forest, I smile, and wonder at God's ways and I am deeply grateful for that precious, difficult time. The stillness was necessary for me. Today I heard an insect move beneath a dead leaf. I stood and listened intently for some minutes. If I had known how to listen more I would surely hear God move too. God has gifted me with preparation time and beauty, which surrounds me.

2nd December, 1982: Yorkville.

I feel I am going round in circles - going into Chicago, looking around, checking out places to live, meeting people, making contacts. Yesterday I spent all day walking around the streets in Chicago. I felt afraid and very small, and I wished I had someone to talk to about that. The streets are cold and impersonal, often dark and frightening. Am I a coward? I had a thought yesterday - just a crazy, selfish thought - of getting on a plane and going home to England. I wanted to run - to disappear - to forget all this. I know I won't - but I know I'll dream and think those thoughts again. I am not so strong and so brave as people think.

10th December, 1982: Yorkville.

THE SHEPHERDESS

I saw a shepherdess
Sitting alone
On a rough grey rock
Overlooking
A vast and misted
Valley.
She stared, as if
Stunned,
At the wreathing fog -
Unsure
Of its secrets -
All that it might hide
And all

It might reveal.
I said
"Where are your sheep?"
She looked up,
Smiled a second and
Seemed sad.
Then brave, and then
Afraid and
Solitary
"Oh, no,
I have no sheep."
She said,
"Not now,
Not now."
I left her,
Still sitting,
Fragile and lost, looking
At the distant
Deep valley,
From afar off,
I turned for that
Last quick glance.
The shepherdess
Was gone.
There was only
A lamb,
Alone and trembling
By the rough, grey rock.

11th December, 1982: Yorkville.

Went out with an old friend from school, Depaul Genska last night.
Depaul, a Franciscan priest, has been a voice crying in the wilderness
on behalf of women in prostitution for over fifteen years now. We
drove around the "red light" areas for awhile. Then, we went to a small
bar, where men come to pick up prostitutes. The only people in the
place were prostitutes and clients. They were friendly. The barman
brought us a drink.

I met Amy, Kelly and Mandy. Mandy especially was talkative and friendly. She is in prostitution to pay for her school fees to study music and opera - a Catholic - goes to Mass occasionally, but not communion because, "What I'm doing isn't right..." My presence obviously caused some bewilderment and after a little while one of the women came up to me and invited me around the back for $50.00. They thought I was looking for gay sex! I feel helpless and out of my depths.

16th December, 1982: Yorkville.

PATTERNS

It is all beginning to fall into place,
All the messy unclear pieces
Tumbling together into
A vague harmony.
I have felt downcast and lonely
But yesterday
God burst into my emptiness
And all my fears dissolved as if
They had never been there.

18th December, 1982: Yorkville.

Christmas is almost here. I love the sense of Christmas - the anticipation and excitement in the air. I love the stores, the lights and the gift buying. It throws into relief the poverty and loneliness experienced by so many. It is hard to ignore these realities at Christmas. Only at this time do people seem to notice the poor at all. After eleven months famine, the poor are overwhelmed by the feast given by people of good will, who are moved to pity at this time. Maybe we find it difficult to enjoy the festive excess of our lifestyles unless we first assuage a deep disturbing sense of guilt at having so much, so at this time we are generous. The Kingdom will be here when we share our resources and blessings at all times. Then there will be no famine and no plenty - just enough for everybody.

I move into Chicago next month. I have rented a room in a Community Center that used to be a convent and is owned by the Sisters of Mercy. It is in "Uptown" - a poor and run-down area of the northside of Chicago.

6th January, 1983: Yorkville.

Afraid! Blind! I still wonder, occasionally, if all this is crazy. "Just believe." - It is enough! "Have faith." - It is enough! It is not necessary to understand or to be enlightened. It is only necessary to have faith. I am beginning to believe that it is not the prostitutes who need the Church, but the Church which needs the prostitutes.

> God sends me to the prostitutes
> Because we, the Church,
> Are so hungry,
> So bewildered,
> So proud.
> We are in need,
> And only the "sinners",
> The prostitutes,
> And those who have no cause
> To be proud
> And self righteous
> Can help us find
> Our way again.....

11th January, 1983: Hermitage, Yorkville.

I have come here to spend a day of prayer in the hermitage. This place and time is a very special gift from God. How I love the silence and the beauty! How I love the forest and the creek! All of it permeates with God's life. The silence has a life of its own - we create it by listening! I pray for this, my new ministry, that much fruit will be

borne. I pray also that I can carry with me into the city, the beauty
and the silence of this forest and the peace of the hermitage.

16th January, 1983: Chicago.

I can't believe I am here. I feel God smiling. What next? Where do I
go? Who do I meet? I must get to know the folk. Walk the streets.

17th January, 1983: Chicago.

I spent a day of walking around, trying to get to know the area and
meet people. I feel I have packed a lot into this first day (and the snow
is thick on the ground!) - but it is good and feels right. I pray a lot as I
walk around. This evening I went to a shelter (a church basement)
where 200 men are given a foam mattress and a blanket, and sleep in
rows like living assembly lines. It was a privilege to be there. In the
brief encounter I felt some communication and a real response to my,
"Welcome Sir, I hope you have a good night!" Hell - a good night!!
But what else is there to say? I then went to the women's shelter. No,
a mixed shelter of maybe 20 men and 16 women. There is nothing but
a cheap hardboard partition between the men and women. What
degradation! A diminishment of God's people! I still ask, "Where am
I going, Lord?" I will not know until the journey ends. Today, I have
encountered homelessness, hunger, poverty, misery. All of it is utterly
depressing. I hope I never get used to this poverty and misery! I hope
it always bothers and disturbs me!

18th January, 1983: Chicago.

We cannot know the God of the guts and the gutters unless we have
travelled deep enough within ourselves to touch and experience our
own guts - where God lives, and unless we have reached out far
enough beyond ourselves to smell and sit in the gutters - where God
squats. Today I was able to recognise and call Rose by name. She is a
'bag lady', and today I found her sitting on the stairs of the train station.
I want to listen to people's stories. Only then do I have a chance to

know them. Who is Rose? What happened to her to bring her to the streets? Does she dream? Does she hope? What is her history? Must we lose her history as we have lost the history of so many women? I hear she was once a university lecturer - certainly, in spite of her confused and garbled conversation, she has an amazing knowledge of history and literature as well as a sharp wit. Rumour has it that the husband she adored, abandoned her. Unable to live with the anguish and the rejection, Rose fled into a twilight world of fantasy. The dark anonymous streets swallowed her up, and here she wanders - her once quick mind anesthetised, soaked in a stupor of misery. But who really knows her story and its pain?

Who knows the stories of women driven to abandon themselves to the streets?

21st January, 1983.

I helped out at the soup kitchen and sat at table with some of the folks. I saw a few familiar faces and made some new friends; Marie, the bag lady who can play the piano with remarkable skill and appreciation. This tattered woman who emanates violence and anger is transformed when playing Beethoven on the old Salvation Army piano. There is Miriam, hard looking and tough...."Teddy Bear", (street name for Dolores) - a Mexican girl who seems to have lots of problems that I can't even begin to imagine. I am aware of being surrounded by broken women who carry in their hearts wounds and bruises too deep to be healed. They are scarred over with years of scavenging on the streets in a desperate attempt to forget and to repress.

I saw Rose again - she has violent outbursts that come out of all the anger she has inside. The women seem to be noisy and expressive and the men passive and silent. Maybe the men are struck dumb and silent by the shock of what they have become. Maybe the women are better at communicating their rage. Maybe they all do it in different, and yet remarkably alike, self destructive ways. What else is there for them? Broken dreams, smashed hopes come back, again and again, beckoning them to death and welcome oblivion.

22nd January, 1983: Chicago.

Went into the thrift store and there bumped into a woman called Muriel. We walked around together for an hour or so before she took me to her basement apartment which she shares with Therese, a young, nervous woman who smokes a pipe. They live in absolute squalor and poverty, sharing it all with a dog and a cat. I wonder how and why people choose to live in such squalor? I know I would have to achieve some order and even a little loveliness in a corner of a basement in order to live and survive. I found it depressing although I am grateful to meet and be welcomed by these women.

Earlier this morning a young girl called Sandy dressed in a grubby bright green jacket, looking untidy and tired, stopped me on the street and asked me for a cigarette. I was glad I had some. We walked together a while and talked a little. If she is not already in prostitution she is ideal material - young, beautiful and poor. I wished so much to be able to talk to her, but I felt the time was not right. I prayed that I might meet her again.

I meet so many women. They welcome me into their squalid rooms, talk to me in the streets, wave at me and ask me for cigarettes, and yet I know nothing of their lives. These women protect their privacy as their only valuable possession. They are transients whose stories are hidden. They cannot trust. Why should they? What has ever been in their lives to teach them to trust? Maybe I will never know their history. I will have to imagine their story so they are more than names to me. I will have to learn to accept them for who they are today, and not who they were or who they could become.

24th January, 1983: Chicago.

I went to the Food Pantry and helped to pack food bags for the folk who came asking for emergency food. It's awful to see people really hungry especially in one of the richest countries of the world. Later in the day I went to the Drop-In Shelter, a ramshackle, depressing place for the homeless who sit and sleep, or watch T.V. There must have been about sixty men there. I sat next to "Gypsy" - an elderly street man who told me his life story of poverty, crime and alcohol. Gypsy is a very gentle, sensitive person who had an abusive childhood. As a boy, his father used to make him kneel without moving on rice grains for hours at a time! His grandfather brewed home-made wine in the basement and introduced Gypsy to drink at the age of three. He has been drinking ever since. Gypsy is proud to say that when he was nine his teacher seduced him and even kept him back a year so he could stay in her class. Because of his small and delicate stature Gypsy was always the one who was made to climb through windows and sneak through houses to unlock doors for gang burgularies. As he grew older Gypsy embarked on his own criminal career but he was not a smart criminal and always got caught. Consequently, he was in and out of jail and eventually, like hundreds of others, found himself wandering the streets of Chicago. As I listened to Gypsy I began to realise how much beauty and potential talent is lost through childhood abuse and lack of opportunity. Gypsy and I talked a lot. He told me he was "rotten", but I told him he was "beautiful". I believe he is. I saw it in his eyes. I was grateful for that time with Gypsy.

Finally, I walked home. It was quiet, and my walk was pleasant...I'm feeling more comfortable with the place now. But, will I ever call it home?

7th February, 1983: Chicago.

I spent the morning with Joyce - who used to work as a prostitute. She first got into prostitution when she needed glasses and could not pay for them. Her optometrist offered them free if she would go to bed with him. It was a tempting option for a single parent struggling to take care of a baby and make ends meet. After that, it became her way to survive poverty. Joyce has put me in touch with May who is a Madam and runs a brothel. I am to visit May tomorrow. I don't know what I could do in a brothel. What can I say? This is getting scary!

I got talking to Elizabeth, another "bag lady" in the streets. "I was a dental nurse once", she said both proudly and sadly. I went with her to visit her friend, Annie, who lives in great squalor in a single room. I found the smell and stuffiness hard to bear. What can I do with such human squalor and loneliness when my whole body rebels against it? To reach Annie we had to climb over mounds of garbage piled up to four feet high in her cockroach-infested room. She sleeps in a corner, covered in garbage. I was welcomed.

On the way back I dropped into the men's shelter and had a chat with Gypsy who introduced me to another street man, Joe - an Eskimo from Alaska. Once street people see you a few times and see you are going to stay around, they are the friendliest folks. There is a street code that commands if you are a "friend", you share whatever you have. Joe, the gentlest of men, claims he has never recovered from having to kill in Vietnam. He has spent most of his days drunk since then.

The women and men I meet are people who do not belong in the streets. They are mentally ill and were thrown back into the community for the community to care for them. They are not dangerous to anyone. They simply cannot cope with conventional day to day living. The myth we are asked to believe is that these men and women are out in the streets because they want to be, or because they are lazy, or don't care. Street people have the same wants and needs I have. They need to be needed, wanted, respected and accepted. Will I learn how much I need them, and let them know?

8th February, 1983: Chicago.

Today I met May in her brothel. Surprisingly, it is a very ordinary, unassuming place. One of a block of apartments. Inside it is quite small and cramped with only two bedrooms which are in constant use. May told me that often there is a line of men waiting for another client to leave. The apartment is filled with huge potted plants and pictures of animals on the wall. There are also pictures of the Sacred Heart and the Virgin Mary, but I suspect she put those up in honor of my visit! I stayed for most of the day. May is old, but zipping with energy and activity. She clearly has "the girls" under full control. She hardly sat down for a minute but was answering the phone, fixing dates with "johns" (the male clients), opening the door, planning the lunch for her women, and today also for me. I sat, drinking coffee and watched it all. The three women who were there today accepted May's matriarchial authority and, in a way, even seemed fond of her. But somehow, it is all so sad. The women have lifeless, lonely eyes and hide their hurt behind masks of hostility, bravado and drunkeness. They sat laughing at the clients and making little of them. I said nothing. What could I say but just sit and listen? We have so few experiences in common - no common language or understanding. Can we ever have a meaningful bonding under these circumstances? Behind the jokes I heard their anger and contempt for the men who buy their time and services. And yet when a client came in they all got up and paraded their bodies, competing with each other for the client. As soon as he disappeared behind a door, the remaining women would continue their derisive comments.

Afterwards my emotions were very mixed. I felt grateful and happy to have been well received and I am free to go again. I appreciate their trust. But I find their lifestyle demeaning. Human beings deserve more. I doubt these women have ever known real love. I am disturbed by my anger and resentment against the johns who were in and out of the house all day. They are, almost without exception, middle-aged, middle-class, professional, married men. Theirs is surely the crime, for they lie, deceive and abuse, beneath a mask of decency and respectability. The women speak openly about who they believe they are and what they are doing. There is no pretence there. There is no double standard here. "We are shit", they freely told me, "the scum of the earth". I winced at their lack of self-esteem.

Once again God has opened a door for me. I dare not think what it will lead to. I feel helpless at this point. I pray that God will touch the hearts and lives of May, (who incidentally claims herself a devout Catholic and goes to Mass every Sunday), Miranda, Catherine and Mary. I pray also that I will be there to see God's touch.

9th February, 1983: Hermitage, Yorkville.

TWILIGHT

See the shadows - blue, transparent,
Gather up the crystal light
Enfold the golden leaves in darkness
Clothe the silver path in night.
And there we walk in constant wandering
From the light into the dark
Through the clear, impelling dawn
Into twilight's taunting shades.
All around us, ever changing
Donning masks and colors new
Breathing gently, crying loudly
Whispering in the startled air.
One thing sure,
Just one thing known
Only God is
Constancy.

Ah, how I love this place! I love rediscovering the simple joy of being here. I had almost forgotten the quality of peace and silence of this place, utterly silent - utterly still. A little place for rest and listening for a few days. I'm intoxicated by the silence and the solitude! Blessed time - even if I only sit and look at it. I need to come back to this place to keep things in perspective. There is so much pain and loneliness on the streets that one could easily go down under if one doesn't keep a balance. How can one absorb so much pain and survive? My role is to absorb some of the pain of the women I am learning to befriend, some of their anger, and not pass it on to another.

I need to allow my faith to transform what I receive so I can return love and nurturing in its stead. I need to have this silence and solitude so the process of conversion can happen within me. Only thus can I survive. It's not only that I have been singled out personally - blessed and chosen to do special work. After all, we are all chosen for something only we can do or be. I have imagination which sees and believes in new possibilities and new horizons, and this imagination allows me to fulfill my history. If I can imagine it, I can do it, if I can imagine me, I can be. I am faithful to my imagination - a gift which all of us have received to one degree or another, but which very, very few of us ever begin to develop. The seeds of the Kingdom of God have always been amongst us - we just don't recognise and fertilize them. Imagination is of God and is a powerful pathway to God.

St. Paul believed that when he was weak then he was strong. Oh - how naively I had always understood that. For a moment, it heartened me and I smiled, and I knew that deep in my guts I do believe it.....That is why I will never give up, not because I am faithful, but because God is faithful.

10th February, 1983: Chicago.

The women talk and I listen:

"I would just do it to hurt myself. I hated my father. It was one way of getting back....Hurting myself maybe would hurt him."

"I was lonely. I had no one to come home to. I had to have someone to come home to. Even a pimp is better than having nobody."

"I switch off. Don't think about it."

"To have someone who really cares....really loves you...just someone who would put their arms around you and hold you.....even if he does beat you sometimes."

"You think you are just a piece of shit. The guys are all pieces of shit...."

"I was never allowed to be my own person. I never learnt how to make decisions for myself. My pimp did everything for me - I didn't have to worry about anything."

"Some people hit food, some people hit drink - when I am depressed and lonely, I turn tricks. What difference does it make?"

"I would never have talked to a person like you. How could I...on welfare and a prostitute, talk to you? Why would you want to talk to me?"

I am learning fast that the women we criminalise for prostitution have as much need as any of us for love and understanding. Often all they get is abuse and jail. Almost all the women I have met and talked to, so far, were abused way back when they were just children. Their world has been one of violence. They have always confused love and abuse and many times equate the two. Why don't we understand?

11th February, 1983: Chicago.

Rose met me on the street corner and asked if I wanted to go to a party. So I said, yes...took half her bags and strode off with her. "Say I'm your friend", she said, as we neared the building. Obviously she was afraid they wouldn't let her in...perhaps she was scared of rejection if she went alone? Anyway we both strode confidently a couple of blocks, like a couple of duchesses, up the stairs and into a huge ballroom where the band was playing and lights flashing. We found ourselves a table and I bought coffee. Then I saw Pat, Charlotte and Arlene, also from the women's Drop-In place. they were pleased to see us and came and joined us. There is a real simplicity and earthiness about the street women. They don't need our masks. I am grateful to be so quickly accepted by them. I think they accept quicker than we in the established communities. Maybe someday one or more of them will learn to trust me and in trusting me they might learn to trust themselves.

From there I went to the soup kitchen. Didn't see too many people I knew, but spent a lot time with Teddy Bear. She is only twenty-seven years old but looks sick, sees no hope, drinks, is depressed....but talks freely. Her history helps me understand her present lifestyle. It seems her mother hated her and for most of her childhood kept her locked up in a small room, where she had all her meals alone and talked to her toys. At 12, Teddy Bear was sent to a boarding school, a reformatory, where, in between many run-aways, she stayed until she was 17. Since then she has lived on the streets very quickly moving, inevitably, into prostitution and drugs. Who wouldn't? I held her as she cried. "I'm scared - so scared", she was sobbing. I prayed for her. Her life is beyond anything but the power of God. I'm so glad God took me there tonight. I feel overwhelmed at so much poverty and pain. I ended the evening at the Street Shelter. Sat with Gypsy again and listened to the supervisor haranguing the men on how they should behave. Again - I am grateful for the acceptance I experience at the Shelter. If I had to go through what most of these guys seem to go through, I would have real problems with white, middle-class established Christians. But, yet again, I wince at their lack of self-esteem, which keeps them seeing themselves as not worth even a greeting. I assume God winces too.

ENOUGH

What do you say?
What can you say?
Why, nothing,
For this is another world
Whose ways are different,
Whose faces are
Awesome,
Full of mystery, and awful knowledge,
And unknown fears.
What is their language?
I cannot speak of
Books and poetry,
Food or fashions.
I cannot debate about
God or morality,
Ministry or celebration.
I can only sit
Dumb and helpless -
A child,
Untutored to a world of
Street and brothel

And shelter.
Their faces are fixed
And silent,
Carved into lines of
Pain
By years of wind and
Snow and dirty sidewalks.
They shuffle, slouch and
Drag themelves from
Shelter to shelter,
And stand in
Weary derelict lines
Outside the soup kitchen,
Where cheery well fed
Youngsters
Excitedly prepare the
Rice and cabbage for
The hungry poor.
An experience.
To feed the hungry -
Just like Jesus said.
They take turns,
Come in bus loads,
Each week
A different group.
But the faces in
The lines are always
The same.
No "experience" for them.
They are not interested in
The hand that
Feeds them,
Only want
To fix that aching belly
With swimming cabbage.
They are silent,
Only the coughs and
Spitting to be heard.
They have learnt

To be silent
Before the stark horror
And bleakness of
Their lives.
Dirty sidewalks,
Swimming cabbage,
The dreary basement shelter.
Ah, great and gentle God!
Will you be silent too?
Or will your Kingdom
Erupt,
Scattering cabbage and garbage
All over the basement floor?
Will you reach out,
Oh, great and gentle God,
Letting your tears
Cleanse and heal
The dirty bodies,
The broken hearts?
Oh, great and gentle God
Will you cry aloud and
Crush the rat and the cockroach?
Will you sob,
"Enough!"
Will you?
Will you?
Great and gentle God.

13th February, 1983: Chicago.

I went out about 4.00 p.m, wondering who God would put in my path. I went into a bar and met Anna, a bag lady, age 53. She started talking to me, took a loaf of bread out of her bag and a tin of tuna fish and asked if I'd like a sandwich. How much more easily the poor share of the little they have! So we sat at the bar eating bread, tuna and a banana....it was very dark and the music was loud. Anna talked. She cried. She said she was lonely and sad....a desperate woman. She talked about men in her life who had used her and left her. She still works as a prostitute and she asked me outright if I wanted to team up and work with her. I didn't know how to respond, but in the end, I told her I was a minister. She didn't know whether to laugh or cry, but eventually decided to cry. Then after a shower of tears, she collapsed and, exhausted, fell asleep on the bar counter. I felt so helpless. There was nowhere to take her - no home - no shelter open. There were only the streets - always the streets. I just sat next to her, surrounded by all the noise and laughter of a bar, and felt so totally inadequate to help or to comfort. I left her a note with the address of the shelter and walked away. In the darkness outside I pondered on how we had broken bread together and eaten together and talked about life and God. We had held each other. Eucharist has been broken and shared in that hellish place.

NOT SO GREAT

The streets, full of despair and garbage,
Lonely frightened people, no work, no home,
No place to go, so keep walking, or hang around
The corners, looking confident and, if you can, cheerful.

When I asked Tom, "How y'doing?" he responded
Heartily, "Oh, great....great...."
And then, - quiet, stumbling, with an awful sadness:
"Well....well....I guess...not so great, not so great."

Bloodshot eyes downcast on the dirty sidewalk,
Until rising, they meet with mine, and in that
Single second of sickening truth, sobs out,
"Not so great, not so great...."

Stumble off Tom - kicking the garbage, hiding
The tears, run - run!
From the awfulness of knowing it is
Not so great, not so great.

18th February, 1983: Chicago.

The compassionate woman sobs before the sadness of it all, sometimes longing to run from the darkness and the dirt and the great loneliness of the streets. She wonders how she can absorb the violence, and its pain, that scars the souls of each person in these dark streets. I must try to understand a little the ways of God. I cannot center on myself but must look out to others and to be open to the work God wants to do through me. I am in need of strength and affirmation and, it will come not from me, but from all these others in whom I experience God.

Joyce and her small son...whose whole life is taking a new direction because God brought me here to invite her to seek a new path.

Gypsy...who is surprised by love because God loved him through me.

Arlene...who told me her story in her poverty-stricken, cockroach-ridden home. I watched the cockroaches crawling in procession over the furniture as she cried.

Teddy Bear....who is so desperate for new life and looks at me for hope.

Mary....so lonely, overdosing herself with tranquilisers to forget the emptiness.

Kathy....who has only ever known physical violence, so frightened of being touched, she winces if you pass too close by her.

May...so confused and afraid for all her anger, violence and screaming.

Rose...trying to be brave as she stands smoking and cursing on street corners.

There are so many. "Lord, let me look at these your people, instead of at myself."

21st February, 1983: Chicago.

I go out each day on the streets - there are so many people with so
many different hungers and so little to hope for. I have to fight against
a sense of helplessness. I spent another night in the shelter. It was
depressing. People respond as they are treated - they measure their
worth or worthlessness by the value that is given to them. When I see
these shelters - run by good and well-meaning volunteers - I see a
vicious circle of poverty - the poor trying to help the poor, sticking
band-aids on broken bodies and spirits. Justice demands that all
people have shelter, food, clothing and a sense of belonging to a
community that has a place for them. But, in these shelters, these poor
and depressing places for a night, the floors are dirty. The blankets
look filthy because they are old and worn, the mattresses are stained
and there are no bath/shower facilities. At 6.00 a.m., in this shelter, we
wake up the weary old and confused young and send them outside with
nothing. They have to wait for hours in the inhospitable world, until
the shelter opens up again for the night. They come back early to
assure their own little corner, or else they may be turned away. No
place is ever saved for them. We have to do better than this! **We can
do better than this!** Sometimes, though, I wish God had not led me
here. I would be more comfortable not knowing, not seeing....

27th February, 1983: Chicago.

I went back to Yorkville and took Teddy Bear with me for a couple of
days. It was good to have her and it gave her the opportunity to rest,
relax and get off the streets. She is a good person, but very wounded
and with no real sense of self worth. Well, I suppose anyone would
have a hard time feeling self esteem if they had spent their childhood
locked up like an animal. Perhaps that is why she is an alchoholic and,
perhaps, the alcohol contributes to the woundedness. She is caught in
a never-ending cycle of self destruction! I pray that she will be free of
alcoholism, a devastating disease. She is intelligent and has a lovely
personality, when sober. It would be yet another tragedy to see her die
on the streets. Only God can crack this one! But I care about Teddy
and hope so much she will make it.

I begin to see and feel the need for a place. Already, God –I am asking for the miracle of a house!! I keep bumping into Gypsy – he's such a gentle and beautiful man. As I walk the streets, befriending the women, I find treasures, hidden behind tired, leathery faces and I can't pass them by. This is surely a mutual ministry –it would be very hard for me if I didn't have the friendship of Teddy and Gypsy. They are my guides in the streets, my teachers of a world that is not mine. Living on the streets is a hard life, but working on the streets is hard too! I am in touch with so much loneliness, poverty and misery, all together, all in one place. To endure the sadness of it all, I have to depend on a very real and deep faith. I hope mine is deep enough, just deep enough. That's my prayer, **"God, gentle God, that my faith is deep enough."**

2nd March, 1983

A full day. Went to my local friendly brothel and spent the morning there. Met Candy, and this time I felt free to talk to her and ask her some questions about her life. Candy is Jewish. During the 2nd World War, her parents and brothers and sisters were murdered by the Nazis, but she was smuggled out of Germany and taken in by a wealthy American family. Although they had money and gave her everything she needed materially –a home and education– they never touched her, held her or loved her. She grew up devoid of any human touch whatsoever. It seems that whilst many women enter a life of prostitution as a result of early child abuse, some take the same path because they have been starved of any physical or emotional contact. The deprivation, it would appear, leads to a craving for bodily contact. Cold, detached and without any feeling, she threw herself into the beds and arms of anyone who would take her. Candy shrugs and laughs emptily, but I think she is a very lonely and frightened person –particularly in view of the fact that she is over 40. There isn't much future for a 40 year-old prostitute! She is a bit puzzled about who I am and what I'm about. This makes two of us!

I also met Irene –beautiful, young, vivacious, extrovert –ready to talk, but forever jumping around and moving about. She has psychological problems and also suffers from epilepsy. Her doctor/psychiatrist came in today, as a "trick"... The Scriptures really come alive for me in this place. "Alas for you, scribes and Pharisees, you hypocrites! You who are like whitewashed tombs that look handsome on the outside, but inside are full of dead men's bones. In the same way you appear to people on the outside like good honest men but inside you are full of hypocrisy." The men retain all the trappings of respectability in society, while the women are criminalized and thrown in jail! My eyes are being opened.

Didn't see much of May - she was quite happy to leave me chatting with the girls. I really do feel quite amazed that I've got into this place at all. It will take time, but eventually - if I am a regular visitor I think I will be accepted and trusted. I still don't know what I can do here. May gave me $20.00 again! this is the second time. It is an irony that my support for this ministry is coming from a Madam, her profits in this system of prostitution. I accept it, conscious of the conflict in me and the confused motivation for giving.

Teddy Bear called tonight at 11.00 p.m. from the shelter - she was drunk again. How can I help her if I have no alternatives to offer her? Where can she obtain a support system? I can only do what I can with my present limited resources, loving her, seeing her when I can, letting her visit. It is all temporary, and not enough. I am beginning to recognise how much the friends and relatives of alcoholics must suffer, they become sick too. I am aware of being caught in Teddy Bear's alcoholism, but I can't help myself. What else can I do?

3rd March, 1983: Chicago.

I took Teddy Bear to hospital for a check-up today, and I spoke to her doctor. Her condition is very serious - she will not survive unless she stops drinking. I really will do all in my power to help Teddy Bear - and God will have to work overtime again.

4th March, 1983: Chicago.

I have arranged with the Sisters here for Teddy to move in and have a room with us. It is a new beginning for her. At least she is off the streets. We met Gypsy and the three of us walked around. I am thinking and talking seriously to people about the need for a place. Teddy's un-met needs have had a great influence on me. In many ways she has come to symbolise the women of the streets. Her early childhood speaks of violence; emotional, physical or sexual. Her history is one filled with uncertainty, lack of love and permanence. She took to the streets as if salvation was to be found there, while instead, she found drugs and alcohol. These hid her misery, her failure, her lack of loving intimacy - they distorted her world....and she survived, through prostitution, masking her feelings each time.

ASH WEDNESDAY

Ash Wednesday in the little brothel -
The Madam cursing and swearing,
Condemning all the hookers as
Liars, cheats, thieves...
"Wouldn't trust any of the
Thieving bastards!"
And on her forehead there is
A large grey smudge -
Ashes from the church she
Went to this morning....

No meat for lunch -
"We're fasting", she proclaims,
Amid curses,
and thumps a plate of fried eggs
On the plastic table cloth.
I try to explain to the women
That fasting in our lives
Does not necessarily mean not eating,
But can be a doing something
For others.

Loving, caring, being there...
And I suggest that May, the Madam
Cut out two of her
Most obscene swear words
For Lent....
The women laugh and
One says,
"May would have nothing left
To say..."
It all seems so ironic
So twisted, so hopeless,
But then,
So did the cross,
And so did
All the human situations
Of sin that
Jesus encountered
Wherever he walked.
How will the Kingdom
Break through into
The brothel?

9th March, 1983: Chicago.

Teddy seems to be blossoming - responding to the love and friendship
which is being extended to her. I pray that she will persevere and
flourish and be the "first rose blooming on the Broadway". Tonight I
left her alone on the streets for the first time in a week. I am a little
afraid for her, but I think she'll make it. Went to May's this morning. I
felt more relaxed and at ease than I have ever been. May, Nancy, Irene
and I talked and joked and actually had a really good time!

I met a "trick", Bob, an ex-priest who demands particularly demeaning
sexual acts. He wanted me to make up a threesome with him and one
of the women. I think he is ill and is playing out all his guilt, fears and
insecurity in sexual fantasy. One of his games shows how he confuses
his boundaries with religion. He likes getting the girls to kneel naked
on the floor and ask for forgiveness while he "blesses" them and prays.

The women do it for him, for the pay they will get. These women take so much abuse. It is painful to be here. Sometimes I can hardly believe I am where I am, hearing what I hear, and seeing what I see. I don't know what I can do, but I am convinced God brought me here and must have a few ideas. The women deserve at least some hope of something other than violence and abuse. All I can do at this time is be here and listen and love these women regardless, or maybe because, of all I hear. What am I getting into?

10th March, 1983: Chicago.

Visited May's again and had lunch there. One of the guys today was in full police uniform. He works in the Sheriff's Office! He is not the only one who comes, I am told. So much for the law, no wonder the prostitutes are as cynical as they are. I am seeing "the other side" and I do not like it.

Went to hospital with Teddy. Great results! The doctor is amazed at the progress. She is like a new woman. Later we talked and Teddy told me she had been in prostitution for years. When she eventually left the residential home (for girls with behavioral problems) in her late teens, she was on her own in the world. With no family support, no friends, or self-esteem, she did the only thing she could do to survive - prostitution. Drugs and alcohol soon followed. Her experience will have so much to give to this ministry. I gave Teddy Bear a journal and suggested she might like to write her story, feelings or anything that came into her head. She was excited.

What next? We must find a house!

PART IV: TEDDY BEAR'S STORY

Teddy Bear: 16th March, 1983. Yorkville.

As I sit here alone in the woods by the stream, I'm thinking back to my childhood. As I can remember I was a lonely, maybe, unloved person. I was mischievous and uncontrollable, always in trouble. I still don't understand yet. I was put away from home by my mother. She couldn't control me as she said, that's when I was twelve and a half years old. I lived in an orphanage home for four months, they put me out, 'cause I was always in trouble. They couldn't handle me either so I went to boarding school, temporarily. I left there on my thirteenth birthday. Went to another boarding-school. I stayed there till I was fifteen and a half. I ran away - the police found me. The boarding-school accepted me back again.

I ran away numerous times and I always came back. When I was seventeen, I lived at the Y.W.C.A. I was all alone, one year went by. All the time I was turning tricks on the side till I met Jeremy. I fell in love. I knew he was a pimp. We went to motels, made love, went to the movies while two of his ladies were out working. Then he talked me into living with him. My Aid check would come and I gave it to Jeremy. I started sniffing heroin. My habit was expensive, so I had to go out and make money for my habit. Then I started the needle. They had me cut off Public Aid.

I left Jeremy and I went back again and again and he would beat me up every time. I left him when I was twenty three-and-a-half years old. I started drinking. I was drinking heavy. I was an alcoholic. Things went bad. Two operations, many times I was in hospital. I tried suicide three times. But now I am living in an entirely different world. I met new friends. Beautiful people. I owe it all to Edwina, who helped me, and also God who helped me love myself and love all my friends. I feel love. I feel beautiful. I feel like a different woman. I'm happy, I'm loved, I don't feel lonely anymore.

I have a son four years old. He's adopted by my mother. I love him, but I don't have him. He doesn't know I am his mother. He was a mistake. His father is unknown. I had him when I was a prostitute on the streets. When he's old enough I hope he will understand. I couldn't give him the time and the love my mother has given him. It hurt at first, but now it's settled down. I have abandoned him now for numerous reasons. One....I couldn't never take him from my mother. It would kill her. God can forgive me.

Things will get better I know. I'm not strong yet. But I'm getting there. Every day I feel a little more stronger.

Love,

Teddy Bear: 25th March, 1983. Yorkville.

Today is Friday. It's just been one of those beautiful days of my life. I felt really good inside. I really felt love inside. I cooked today with a little help from Edwina. I did a little reading in the prayer service. It was just beautiful. All of us were there, Edwina, Su, Gail, Tom and David; also Chris and Anne - all the VMM community. We all had dinner together. What made it more beautiful, we all had love within each other. We talked. Laughed. I need them, and they need me. They are like a family....which they are my family and Edwina and I are getting an apartment flat with a dog and a cat and just think I'll have my own room. I can just see it now with a backyard, with plants and flowers and little bird house. Then in one year we'll have a great big house.

Love,
    Teddy Bear.

Teddy Bear: 27th March, 1983.

I wonder how it will be to be back in Chicago, because I feel I am a changed person. But I will always be Teddy Bear and also I will never forget about the two weeks I spent out here in Yorkville. It's been the most exciting time of my life, and I know it will be more days like it was.

Thank you Lord
Thank you for sharing
This beautiful life
You've given me.
Love,

Teddy Bear.

28th March, 1983.

Back in Chicago, after a few days away, it seems as if nothing has changed much. Or...is it my imagination that some of the folks on the street look thinner and sicker? The day shelters are such depressing places - but what have these people got to celebrate? Even so - I wish I could bring some joy or sparkle into the daily events of just sitting in these dingy places.

I long so much for a place where this new ministry can find a home. I also have been concerned for Teddy and her needs...yesterday she relapsed and drank. I'd left her on the streets - and she said she gave in under peer pressure. I felt so dejected - she was sorry. It chipped off my confidence considerably, and I trembled as I recalled what people say, "It's almost impossible....they always go back to drink...." I had thought Teddy was unique, different. But, it is not fair to put that on her. I still believe in miracles...but, perhaps, they need more human co-operation and understanding.

Please, Lord, show me the house you have chosen....

29th March, 1983.

I grieve for all I am called to be and am not.

Teddy Bear: 30th March, 1983.

I feel inside my heart that I'm capable of doing anything. I feel good

knowing that I'm cared for because I know that there's God watching
me. I have a mind of my own. There's not anybody who can say,
"Teddy do this, do that, it's not possible." I am happy to be alive, not
just alive but well. Good health and also loved. That's what we need,
to love each other - not be condemned.

Teddy Bear.

1st April, 1983: Good Friday.

I am still looking around for a place...I don't know whether God would
have us in an apartment or a house - rented or bought. Talk about
groping in the dark! But it is such a great joy to see Teddy blossoming
- her doctor can't believe it - she is transformed. Surely the miracle of
Teddy has to be followed with the miracle of the house?

Joyce is also experiencing new life - she is struggling to find herself
and needs a lot of help and support. She is only just managing on
welfare, but has hard times. Her baby son has had a lot of small
infections and does not seem to be developing as fast as he should.
Joyce is nervous and unsure about how to take care of him. She is
terrified to speak to anyone in case they find out about her past life.
How can these women begin a new life when the past pursues them so,
and colors everything they do?

GOD'S MIRACLE

God never ceases to fill me with wonder -
Where am I going?
What is he/she creating?
Only, that it is surely to be
Most beautiful
Bursting with miracles.
Hope - life.
Death.
New growth.
The great birth. Ah! At last!

4th April, 1983.

A doctor rang to say he had heard about me from Teddy's doctor. He asked if I could meet and help a woman called Carol, a native American. I spent a couple of hours talking with her. Like so many dis-placed persons - especially indigenous peoples - Carol turned to alcohol as she saw her native American Indian family disintegrate through poverty, loss of cultural identity and alcohol. This area of Chicago has a large native American population - most of them "living on the fringes" of society. They have lost their roots, their pride, their ancestry. Without a sense of identity or belonging, there is little motivation to do much more than barely survive. Carol is barely surviving. But she is not ready to be helped or to quit drinking. It was sad, but she left. Later that day Teddy and I saw her in the evening, totally drunk. Teddy spent some time with her and that was very good. She said she wanted to go to her sister's, so we walked her down the street. We left her going into a liquor store. "Well," Teddy said, "you can't help everybody!"

Teddy Bear: 8th April, 1983.

The day was special. I learned a lot. I saw a lot. Heard a lot. I talked to God. I listened to Him. I sat there and thought to myself and I said, "What is it that I am afraid of? I'm loved, I'm cared for. I have someone who loves me. I have a community of family and I have someone to teach me everything I don't know. I want to learn who God is. I know some. But not everything. I have so much to learn and understand. But I think I have a little idea."

Teddy.

13th April, 1983.

I walked the streets all day long and hung around the shelters and the bars feeling lost. I drove around dozens of houses but it is difficult because I don't really know what I am looking for. But I do know I must have a house where people can be welcomed. Should I buy?

Rent? Wait for someone to give? I have to trust that if I follow my instinct and pray I will do the right thing and God will see to all. Sometimes I wish things were a little clearer and that I knew what I was doing or where I was going. But surely, Teddy herself is enough sign and affirmation?

18th April, 1983.

Teddy is blossoming. So is Joyce. We are praying for a house. The dream becomes a need. The need becomes apparent as I get involved in street life.

Teddy and I walked around with Eskimo Joe today - no sign of Gypsy. We met a lot of folks on the street - Richard and Wayne - both just out of prison. Irish Patrick was very drunk and I drove him down to his hotel room. I don't know where he would have ended up otherwise.

Teddy and I spent a few hours at the Lake while I worked on the proposal for Catholic Charities to fund the house. Both Teddy and Joyce have written supportive letters - they are very beautiful and convincing - more than anything I could have written. Will the Church listen to the prostitutes?

Ah - the Roses on the Broadway!!

Teddy Bear: 18th April, 1983.

I'm in a confused way now. I don't know which way to start. I'm frightened because I want to do it right, and scared I might go at it the wrong way. I'm thinking deeply about it. There's so much to do and I know I am not that strong. I'm hoping I won't go out of my mind and do something I will regret. No, I won't! I will pray. I will not go backwards. And I will not drink. Because drinking won't solve anything. There must be another way. I must pray, pray more harder.

The Lord will let me know which way to go and He will give us our house. I don't know if I'll get any sleep tonight. But I will try.

Teddy.

20th April, 1983.

I have been deeply touched by the faith and the trust of three of the 'poorest' people of God. Teddy, who with quiet confidence said, "Don't worry, we are going to get a house. I know we are –God told me."

Joyce, who said much the same, "of course."
Arlene, who when told to make a wish as she blew out her birthday candles, wished nothing for herself, but a house for us...

Their faith is beautiful to feel. God is treating me with great love. She is truly the Great Mother.

24th April, 1983.

Teddy said, "It's good to be sober. I feel things and see things I have never felt or saw before..."

She has come a long way very quickly and she seems to be aware of what is happening to her. We walked and met Candy working the streets. She looks all broken down, but puts up a tough exterior. She was kicked and three of her ribs were broken this week, and is out on the streets again already. She could barely walk. Well, it was a blessing that we were able to stop and spend a few minutes listening to her. The seed is sown –at least one life-line thrown out –taken or not.

Teddy and I found two homeless women, Stella and Judy, trying to sleep in the doorway of a church late last night. I was able to offer them rooms for the night, here in the community center, thanks to the community's generosity. But it should be every night. There should be no homeless people where there are real Christians. There's some sort of paralysis and apathy in the church - the poor, it seems, are not always with us, if we can possibly avoid it. In the early church people were asked to sell all they had and give it to the poor before they joined the community. How come so few of us hear that mandate anymore?

STELLA

I found her scrunched up -
Like a polyester ball,
On the church steps.
It was April and cold,
And well past midnight.
Her grey hair was dishevilled,
Like her face,
And her torn pop-socks
Had fallen in little bunches
Around her ankles
She clutched her large plastic bag
Filled with garbage,
Made precious by possession.
"Where are we going?"
She cried,
As she clutched my hand,
And her garbage,
Scuttling bowlegged, along
The dirty street.
Ah, Stella -
Tiny, deaf and toothless -
Away, away from the "house of God"
And the shame of your bed on its steps.
Away, away from this dark smelly street,
That's become your home and bedroom.
Away, away from the passers-by
Looking the other way,
In dark, embarrassed ignorance.
Ah, Stella, Stella

Tiny, deaf and toothless,
Away, away from a church unworthy
Of your precious, precious garbage....

5th May, 1983.

NOSTALGIA

What would I like for my birthday,
You ask?
Oh - I would like to see
The Cathedral tower
Rise above the sloping streets joining
The neat rows
Of English houses.
I would like to see the fields of
Yellow daffodils -
In which I stood, a charmed
And budding poet,
In my teenage years,
Dreaming of fame and art and
Poetry -
Distant lands.
Oh - I would love to walk again
Along the banks
Of Lancaster canal.
Stand - in wonderment before the herd
Of silent, solid cows,
Chewing the cud
By the green flowing water.
Oh - I would love to see
The young duck and cygnet
Lining up behind their splendid
Mothers - proud queens of
Our water-ways.
Oh - I would like to see the
Ancient oak tree,

Rooted in the soil and history of my
Small island home.
Oh - I would like to stand and watch
The morning mist rise from
The wet rich fields around
My city town.
And I would like to hear the church bells
Ringing -
Wondrous sounds -
In Sunday's dawn,
Rousing the devout
And the drunk alike.
Oh - I would like to smell
The odor of plastic,
Bellowing from our local factory's
Chimneys-
Proud to be producing
For a wider world.
Oh - I would like to see
A red double-decker bus
With a conductress
Like my mother,
And on the front, in clear letters,
"MORECAMBE",
Where I used to sell shrimps and cockles
On the sea front.
What would you like
For your birthday?
Oh - I would like
To come home again
For, you see,
I am not
A saint.

Teddy Bear: 6th May, 1983.

I see many things when I see someone. I can feel their pain because I see myself when I was out prostituting. Another thing, when I went into that bar I saw Elizabeth, and when I'd seen her I thought of myself when I was going in the bars. It was like a flash-back. I took her outside of that bar. Just for a minute or two Edwina and I talked to her. Glad to see her anyways. I walked slowly back to the Street Center. I felt hurt and lonely for Elizabeth. We couldn't do anything for her but love her and have concern for her that minute or two. I looked all around the center at the people. I said to myself, they're not happy. They're lonely and need to be loved. When I was drinking I used to think I was happy and then loved. When I was drinking, I thought everything was just fine. Oh, how wrong I was. The guys on the streets are starting to respect me now.

Teddy Bear: 9th May, 1983.

Today is my twenty-eighth birthday. We celebrated Sunday with Edwina's friends. I had presents. It was the greatest party I ever had in my life. I even wore a long dress. Everyone was surprised the see me in a long dress. I was very happy. I felt very special. I also felt so happy. I cried.

Teddy.

12th May, 1983.

LET ME, GOD

My God,
Let me just be faithful.
Let me just be available,
So that you can do
Your mighty works.
We are old friends.

We have walked together
For as long
As I can remember.....
You have taught me,
Led me
Shown your face to me.
Just now
Let me walk faithfully,
By your side,
Gently,
And in
Great confidence.
Let me watch
The creation of your
New Jerusalem.

14th May, 1983.

Spent some time at May's. A new girl, Sandra was there. She's Greek, a little withdrawn and independent. When one of the tricks - Bob - came, she refused him. He asked me then and I refused him too! He sat and talked to me.

It was the first time my heart went out to the trick. He was humiliated. But more than that - deeply hurt, I felt. His pain was so clear. He began to tell me again of how he was once a priest - he obviously has a deep guilt about it. How he must despise himself!! I asked him if he thought about the priesthood often. He said, "All the time." He has not "forgiven" himself so he indulges in self-hatred. He lives out his personal destructiveness throught prostitution, through which he acts out his own prescribed personal and sexual abuse. He punishes himself for "his sin". He pleaded with me to go with him. I knew he was desperate and it made our moment of human contact so, so sad. He said to me, "You look so calm and peaceful". He was grateful for an oasis. He appreciated that I had seen through his tough and aggressive facade and seen the hurting little boy screaming for help. I said, "Maybe that's why you came today. Maybe that's all you needed." He thought for a moment and then said, "Perhaps you're right." He almost cried. So did I.

I began to feel that it is important to love the men as well - in spite of my anger and abhorrence. They too, are wounded, or they would not be coming to the brothel.

May hides her terror and fear of illness in talk and activity. "They're all liars and cheats", she says. Whilst she burns with anger and scorn, she is also generous and kind to a fault. She cares for me and protects me, even in humor. She told a trick that he couldn't have me, "She's got gonhorrea!", she said. (Well, at least it got me off the hook!) Poor May, she is so afraid of her ill-health. She never gives herself a moment to look at herself, to be alone with herself. This brothel is full of pain and anger and fear. All I can do is be in the middle of and pray that God will work the miracles. Teddy continues to blossom. She becomes more alive and more outgoing every day. I continually thank God for the gift of her life and companionship.

Teddy Bear: 14th May, 1983 (Yorkville).

As I look back in my past childhood, I was not happy at all. It has just been a few months ago when I started to be happy. Now I can smile and laugh. Not a fake laugh or smile, but one really meant deep down in my heart. And also I can love again and not be scared to love anyone, and can be loved back. That fear is about all gone. I'm starting to know myself. I never knew myself before. I never gave myself that time or chance before. When I go back in my life when I was on drugs and a prostitute I was so stupid to let my life go to shit. That was one hell of an experience, but my life is so different and beautiful.

Teddy Bear: 17th May, 1983.

I feel very good. I walked two-and-a-half to three hours. It felt good to walk. It took something out of me. I thought a lot while I was walking. It's so different here. It's like walking in another world. It's not like anything I can compare to Uptown. There's nobody to bother you here. It's clean and fresh. The people very friendly and warm. I saw horses and roosters and I even seen a racoon. There were many squirrels. I walked through a forest preserve. I saw many different birds. It was very huge, especially the trees. I met two dogs. Nature can be so beautiful!

Teddy Bear: 18th May, 1983.

I think back on how I misused my body. How I let all them men use my body and mind?   I was so dumb. I can't blame anyone but me. Because I was the one that got into bed with them. That is one scar that won't heal on its own.

Teddy Bear: 19th May, 1983.

Sometimes I wish I was in top of big mountains, hundreds of miles up in the sky, that I could see everything from the top of those mountains, and no one could reach me because it would take them months to get there. I wonder if it's an escape?

If it is, that's where I would go and hide. No one would find me. No one but God would know where I'm at. I would not leave there unless God tells me it's time to go. I wonder if I make sense? I think I do.

Teddy

20th May, 1983.

Today I am 40! I feel very blessed and deeply at peace. I wonder if anyone could feel as blessed as I do. I ponder and gratefully accept all that has been given to me, especially these past nineteen years of ministry. I have received more than a hundredfold - yes, more than a thousandfold. And yet, I always ask for more and more... Everything that I have ever prayed for has been given to me - and more besides. I am spending this day in the forest - I cannot think of a better and richer way to spend most of my 40th birthday. For here I am with God in a special way - here in the hermitage where She taught me faith and perserverance, here where She sowed the seeds of this new ministry, here where I waited in the silence - and heard. The forest is beautiful. It is God saying, "This beauty is my gift for you." It is all around me. I am not to hold and possess it, but to be in it.

23rd May, 1983.

LAKE SHORE

This morning, I went out early, to walk along
the lake front, and through the narrow park land,
straddling the water's edge.
I passed hurriedly by the sleeping humped bodies,
half hidden beneath bushes, and curled around tree trunks.
The sun was rising -
waking the homeless derelict
with gentle light, and the morning chorus
of a dozen birds.
Gentle, compassionate, experience.
Feeling of Wholesomeness -
we are all together under
nature's gentle awakening....
That night I stood by my
bedroom window, watching
the lightning flashing over the
city, feeling the beat of the rain,

and hearing the roar of
cracking thunder.
And in my mind's eye,
I saw the writhing, weeping bodies,
drenched in the night rain, shivering
beneath the rolling thunder,
feeling the wet and sticky earth
seep through tattered jackets and
thinning soles.
I saw the weakest and the poorest,
tossed and sodden,
in the parks where we play.

25th May, 1983.

Today was a difficult day. Teddy got turned down for Welfare after
being kept on a string for nearly two months. I am appalled by the
injustice and by the bureaucracy which makes it almost impossible for
a woman like Teddy to have any alternative but streets and
prostitution. Our bureaucracy treats the poor as a file with a number,
without any regard for their real needs or any sensitivity for their
humiliation. Well - we shall fight them.

I think Teddy feels humiliated and ashamed, and does not want to go
on. It is not suprising! Our societal system puts its people in an almost
impossible situation - no aid, no jobs, no rent money! What do they
do? Go out on the streets - get involved in illegal activities - get
picked up and condemned. This allows society to feel self-righteous
and affirmed in their judgement that these people need no help. It
becomes easy to believe that they bring it all on themselves. Society
does not have to cope with guilt - there's always the scapegoat.
Scapegoats don't win. They can't win. Society can't win.

I spent some time at May's. There was only one woman working -
Juanita. Four or five guys came. Bob came by again, and got very
angry when he didn't want Juanita and there was no one else. We
didn't talk today. John and Peter, two Greeks, came. John is a
professional musician and obviously doing very well for himself. He

is married and loves his wife but thinks it okay to cheat once or twice. Peter, the handyman, talks about his cat. It's all very depressing really! I think May is getting panicky because she hasn't got enough girls.

Still no word from Catholic Charities for funding.

Dear God, don't put us to the test....

2nd June, 1983.

Teddy is at Welfare. She just phoned me to tell me they have kept her waiting four hours so far. I wrote them a letter and we're hoping that it might reverse their previous decision. But what happens to the just cases who have no champion? What happens to those who have no "respectable" citizen to write on their behalf? The people with petty power treat these poor without dignity or respect. I wince to see the humiliation. I know that most petty officials feel humiliated themselves and they become the worse offenders, but how do we break this chain?

I continue to try to push Teddy to some "discipline" and task in her life - sometimes I worry a little that so much "good" has happened to her in such a short time and I wonder if we can maintain a sense of urgency and reality in her life. I don't want Teddy to be so suffocated with goodies and attention that she confuses what we are about. She is intelligent and has a good deal of understanding, so maybe I shouldn't worry. It is God who takes care of her, not me. No news yet regarding the house. We continue to believe and to pray. Stella is staying with me at the community center - at least temporarily. The sin of her homelessness cries to God. These streets are full of despair and fear. The Christian community sleeps on.

I spent time at May's and met Belinda, aged 24 yrs. She also works at a strip club - one of those peep show affairs. The men pay $1.00 for two minutes. Belinda spends most of the time sitting at the kitchen table putting on purple eyeshadow. May was tired and tense. It is a sad house. Catherine hopes and dreams, and talks about the day she'll do something else, so her daughter, Sandra (now two years old) will not have a mother who is a prostitute.

Teddy Bear: 3rd June, 1983.

I feel great. Still waiting on our house. I accumulated a little for my first room. I'm so happy. I want to do so much for our house. I will try my best helping Edwina in our street ministry 'cause there is a need. It will be a struggle, especially for me. I'm starting to talk a little more and also responding. I need to be more open about myself and also talk more. There is so much I know I can talk about, because I have experienced a lot, especially in the streets.

Teddy Bear: 5th June, 1983.

We are going to Boston. I'm really excited and nervous, but happy. I wonder how it feels to be in another State legally? The only time I was in another State before was as a runaway! I will know when I get there. It will probably be no different. I know it sounds a bit silly. I don't know if I should bring along my two bears with me. They might laugh or think I'm strange. Anyway, I think I will bring them. Who cares anyhow?

Teddy.

6th June, 1983.

Gypsy, Eskimo and Stella spent the weekend with us in Yorkville. it is good to see them relaxing - feeling more at home, showing an interest in things. I am so glad that at least I can offer them a little hospitality. I am grateful to my VMM community of lay missionaries. Africans and Papua New Guineans have taught us well about sharing. The Ugandans with whom I worked all those years ago are still influencing my life. What I share now with the street people is only a little of what I first received myself from my African hosts years ago.

Stella is so happy now that she has a bed. She is already beginning to show a little interest in herself and her appearance. What a difference a little joy and a little security brings to people's self esteem. We still need to watch her, so she doesn't fill her pockets with left-over food which then rots in her bags. She still is not sure where the next meal will come from. Yesterday I found two cheeseburgers in her coat pocket....

7th June, 1983.

I do not want to spend precious time begging for dollars. So, God, do not let me be drawn into concern for money when I feel called to be with your people.

Ministry is fulfilled because it is God's and not because it is dependent on anything else. The believing community saw to Jesus' needs because of the witness of his life. It is enough to minister and to believe. The rest will follow.

God of surprises
Give it to us -
The house, the funds,
And we
Will give you our lives.

12th June, 1983.

Teddy and I are spending a few days in Boston. It's very exciting for Teddy - the flight, the new people, the ocean, she is lapping it all up and it is good to see her so happy. A child is emerging in Teddy - the child that was never allowed to be before; her life has been one of constant pain, loneliness and rebellion. This emerging child is so open and spontaneous and excited about life and new possibilities. God, too, must be very excited. I realise more and more, that I need someone to share with, and to dream with, I need another dreamer to encourage me. At times, I have found myself wishing to return to

England and work. I am tempted to believe it would be much easier. And yet I know one is never a prophet in one's own land. Haven't I been always called to leave my house?

Teddy Bear: 12th June, 1983. Boston.

They all seem to be enjoying themselves. I feel more relaxed on my own. They're so different than me. Their whole lifestyle is so much different than mine. But they're no different than I. They make me feel like I'm somebody and not a nobody. I don't understand what came over me, one minute when I was downstairs, I was talking, sharing about myself. Then Bang!! I was quiet and sorta depressed, and I kinda walked away. To be alone and by myself. I guess it's just me, and I cannot change that. I wonder if this is really me? (It must be?)

Teddy Bear: 13th June, 1983.

God please give us a house soon. So I can have my own room. There are so many other women that need our help and love. And I know you want these women to be happy and loved!

So I pray again!
Lord, please
Give us our beautiful house
that you have chosen for us
I love you......

Teddy.

16th June, 1983.

I am facing a few setbacks - Teddy lost her Welfare elegibility again because she failed to complete some form....Carol walked out of the hospital, is drinking on the streets again....Joyce is in a state, and sounds as though she is falling apart....etc.

I am mad with God, but it really comes out of my frustration at not having a place of our own. I know I was very lucky to find a couple of rooms in this convent, so close to where my new friends roam the streets. I sleep in this room, one of many in this corridor, while they sleep in an alley, one of many down this street. I share a meal with the sisters while they share their meager bread and tuna fish or whatever else they have managed to find. We need a place which the women will learn to call HOME - where they will know they are welcomed without having to ask. It would take the pressure off to have our home - always welcoming me and Teddy as well as others.

I don't know what God is doing, but I can't stay mad for too long. I will continue to trust and believe. But I wish She would make it all a little easier.

I went to May's and spent the afternoon there. There was only Catherine and May. Catherine is a beautiful woman with dark eyes and long brown hair. She lives a life of quiet abuse and frequent beatings masked by her calm and gentle looks. She has a two-year-old child, and a husband whom she keeps on cocaine at $200.00 per day. She also pays $35.00 a day for the hotel room where they live. Whilst Catherine is here at May's trying to make the money, Peter takes care of the baby. I shudder for what the child experiences. If she were to go straight, Catherine would first have to break her dependency on Peter which would mean leaving him. "Then," she protested, "who would take care of the baby while I work?" She feels it's a vicious cycle - says she could leave Peter but what else would she do - babysit for seven days a week? The long hours that Catherine puts in at May's pays for rent, food etc. She also hopes one day to return to school and eventually get "straight". But she has to deal with a lot of obstacles before she gets that far.

I wish we had our house so I could invite her over to eat and talk. God - get on with it!!

"Dear God, don't let me become impatient with you. I know you have it all in hand. At the right moment it will come. Help my unbelief."

21st June, 1983.

Teddy got drunk. For the first time in four months she went out onto the streets and drank herself silly. I drove back to Chicago and found her waiting, incoherent, weepy and intermittently aggressive and childish. She clearly needs more help, she is still too fragile and insecure. And I thought she was so strong - I was sure she would make it. I have allowed her to become too dependent on me, now it seems she can hardly function without me. So, we will have to start all over again. I shall have to find ways of helping her grow strong without breaking her. I need to learn more about alcoholism. I feel quite devastated. In some ways I have failed, but I am learning. I am struggling to be compassionate whilst also dealing with my feelings of great anger and disappointment. Have I gone wrong somewhere? It is tempting to feel that all is lost and destroyed. But I will not give up. I feel bruised and a little wiser. I realize that this ministry is not possible without community, and that, maybe, it would be too much to expect of Teddy to want her to be my community support. She is so busy fighting her own internal battles.

Teddy Bear: 21st June, 1983.

I just got in. It's three-thirty in the morning. I walked the streets most of the night. I got back to the community center at 9.10 p.m. It was very dark. No lights. I didn't see no one. There was completely nobody. I was all alone. I should have called Edwina but I did not. I went out. I seen nobody. Could not find anyone. I was alone again. Tried to be strong. I walked the streets. I knew it was wrong of me to stay out this late. I promised to Edwina that I wouldn't be on the streets late. But I didn't keep my word. I will do what I have to do in the morning. Public Aid. I'm very sorry but mostly all alone. I keep trying to do something, I think of Edwina. I love her so much. She's the best friend I have! I'm crying right now.

Oh God, can I make it another day?

Teddy.

28th June, 1983. Yorkville.

The VMM community is very supportive of Teddy. We all sat together and Teddy was able to talk a bit about what happened. She knows she is loved. Most of all now she knows that our love is not dependent on her behavior but that we love her for herself whether she is strong or weak.

Community is vital - a loving understanding community to nurture people into believing in themselves. I have been able to do much alone - but it is still not enough. Someone like Teddy needs others also to affirm her. I too do not know how I would have endured these days without the support of the VMM lay community. We have in common our desire to reach out crossing barriers of race, class, culture and embrace people as brothers and sisters. Teddy is perceived as a sister.

29th June, 1983.

Teddy, Stella and I are back in Chicago. This relapse may bear fruit - it has helped Teddy realise that she is not healed all the way yet, so hopefully, she will be more careful. She has come a little further in self knowledge and acceptance. Also, and most important, Teddy knows she is loved in spite of her relapse. We had a wearying day going to six different places to get all the documentation required (yet again) for her to get on Welfare. If someone already lacks self confidence, the humiliating, time-consuming task of getting on Welfare is surely guaranteed to dispel any last bits of belief they might have in themselves. I know Teddy would never have made it alone without my pushing. That is why so many street people would not consider Welfare as an option. It should not be like that. I am saddened by the utter lack of humanity I have observed and experienced in the system. The poor are treated like shit. Is it surprising that they never or rarely step out of the gutter?

I trust that God is going to give us all we need. I am drawing on my own meager savings and still trusting. It would be so nice to have a home - a place to make into home. This first year has been so fluid and unfocused. It is difficult to live like that all the time. The insecurity of not being able to pin anything down or plan anything is hard. For someone like me, who enjoys having a target and who needs to "achieve", it is especially difficult. God will not stretch me further than I can go. I am trying to leave a lot of space for God. It's hard to get a hold of empty space, and even harder to live in the empty space.

30th June, 1983.

Teddy drank again tonight. I waited for her until 11.30 p.m.,and then went out and found her with a gang of guys drinking on the street. Ah well, Lord, I did try.

It was a hard day all round. It started with my car windscreen smashed in and some of the bodywork scratched. Gypsy came to the door all agitated and distressed, to tell me. Then the day followed with a series of phone calls - police, garage, insurance etc. Oh what a mess!

In the afternoon I went to May's. Irene came for May to take her photo because she had been terribly beaten up by her pimp and was taking him to court. She had to have pictures of the bruises before they began to disappear and heal. It was awful to see her like that - all bruised and swollen up. Dave brought Irene along. Dave is a middle-class married man, now a grandfather with a bevy of grandchildren, and a secure, apparently happy home life of domestic bliss. Another "whited sepulchre" living a double life! He enjoys "young prostitutes who have black pimps". He has become a rich man through stealing - "but only through contractors". He is over 70 and appears pleased with himself that he can step in and pick Irene out of the gutter. May told me, "there is an animal in every man." When I see some of these guys - I believe it.

May has a favorite line: "Meet 'em, fool 'em, leave 'em." She follows that with the quip, "What do you think I'd do without all this excitement in my life? I'd die of old age!" Maybe May would! She is already in her early '70s, still going strong and quite capable of making a couple of hundred dollars herself some nights. Quite a character! She told me some of her stories this evening - mostly about the masochism demanded by some of her clients in the past - "respectable" professional men with families who paid her substantial sums for the privilege of tying them up and beating them or of acting out a "mommy" and "naughty boy" game in which "mommy" smacks the child constantly. Perhaps these men are so repressed at living lives of apparent success and power they are desperate to feed a need deep within them to be small and helpless. These men need some sort of treatment for their psychological imbalance. May told me that she only survived by imagining dollar bills in front of her whenever she was with these men playing games. She would shut the reality out and only visualised the end result - the money. She does not allow herself to stop and think. Or maybe she can't anymore. She told me she was often lonely. She would have had a lot of love and kindness to share and give if she had not fallen into such anger and bitterness. She must have been badly hurt once upon a time. I don't know. She will protect her privacy.

All these women seem to live on two (at least two) different planes. One is the now, everyday life, which involves their fragile ego in the reality of our society. Here they are open, honest, calling each move by name, whether it is theirs or the hypocritical moves of their pimps, johns or any other member of the established society. Then there is a deeper plane, one that from childhood, has been filled with oppression, violence, lack of love, incest, murder etc. Sometimes there is some good memory that needs to be hidden, lest the fresh air soils it - but for the most part they protect, hide, defend the ugly memories from surfacing, because they "know" how these memories can destroy their own fragile sense of self.

Well, I can only be a friend to May in the here and now. "Come and hear me swearing," she said on the phone. Well, at least she invited me! Ah, but it is hard for these women to have so many messy painful things going on all at once. Teddy, May, Irene - all of them face uncertainty. I too, must face my uncertainty - the car, the finances, the not hearing from Catholic Charities. It all seems such a mess. It was a year today that I began my thirty-day retreat. It was such a spiritually intense time. Would I have lived through it if I had known where it would lead me and how confused it would leave me? I don't know whether I would go through it all again.

I must remember all the good things that have happened - meeting May, Catherine and the women. Coming to know and love Teddy, helping her live again in spite of the relapses. Getting to know Gypsy, Joe, Stella and so many other street people.

Of course, the question in my mind is, "Am I making much difference?" Deep down inside of me, and especially stirred with Teddy's relapses, is that uncomfortable little doubt, whether all this is right for me? What am I doing? Am I doing more good than bad? Should I quit and leave this to another, better able to handle alchoholism, finance, homelessness? Please Lord, give me some real affirmation.

1st July, 1983.

Tonight I visited Irene. She still looks terrible after her beating - a guy called Johnny was sleeping naked on her bed and another prostitute, Sylvia, young, black, sharp, was there too. Irene was drunk. She had stolen whiskey and cigarettes which she does often... She talked, cried, argued, denied she was an alcoholic. She said time and time again, "I'm so scared. I'm so scared."

Sylvia talked a lot but in a somewhat garbled hysterical fashion. She was into the drug scene for which she was, no doubt, prostituting. Her husband was shot and killed in April. She too was shot but recovered. The newspapers and TV run almost daily reports on shooting incidents (drugs, robbery cases) in the poor areas of this great city. "Cupcake", another young prostitute, came bursting in and threw water on the sleeping Johnny. She and Irene began to scream and fight. What am I to do in the middle of all this brawling - all this pain and anger? When Cupcake left Sylvia and Irene began to argue. Then Sylvia left and Irene began to cry...

Mess, mess, mess - these womens' lives are so screwed up! God, what are we to do? I came home at midnight and Teddy was waiting for me outside the church and she was in good form....so I don't know what to do with it all. It feels right that I am here!

THE STREETS

I saw the Spirit rising
From the garbage in the street,
And I heard the steps of Jesus,
In the wino's dragging feet.

In the whorehouse I found Mary,
Sitting silent and alone.
And watching, in shame and anguish,
I dropped my first cold stone.

The naked pimp was Lazarus,
Stretched on the dirty bed,
And I looked around for Jesus,
To raise his drunken head.

Down the alley shuffled the bag lady
Foraging and moaning
But she could not find a hem to touch
No Christ to still her groaning.

In screams from crumbling tenements,
Behind broken window panes,
I heard the cries of Israel,
Across Sinai's desert plains.

And I called aloud to Yahweh,
"Oh, hear your peoples' sighs!
Be silent and deaf no longer,
To the anguish of their cries."

Teddy Bear: 3rd July, 1983. Yorkville.

Today been a very beautiful fun day. I was very happy today. Went to church. Had a beautiful brunch. Went to the parade. I felt very happy and really enjoyed myself. The community and I had a great day. No problems at all. No loneliness. No fear of depression at all. Just laughter. There is a tornado watch. The wind is very strong and loud, but I know the community is here all around me so I have no reason to be scared, and also their God is right beside me. I'm so happy that my Public Aid came through. I feel a little bit more dependent on myself. There's so much that I and the community accomplished in the six months that I have known and lived for and share with:

1. Community.
2. Love.
3. Beauty.
4. The Lord.
5. A community center.
6. Beautiful friends.
7. A place to sleep.
8. Eat - Food.
9. Public Aid.
10. Health.
11. Sobriety.
12. Companionship.....and much more.

I'm so grateful. Most of all I have Edwina. The best that could happen to me. Thank you, Lord.

Teddy.

4th July, 1983.

It has been hard for Teddy. Miracles are not so simple and instantaneous as I thought. Teddy needs to deal with her own inner fears and scars before she is whole. It cannot come from outside influence or from new choices she is making alone - that can only be a motivating and supportive influence. The real healing comes from within herself - and she has not yet given it enough attention. For me it is both disheartening and instructive. Disheartening because I had thought we were further than we are and that Teddy was stronger than she is, and instructive because I need to learn to walk at her pace and not mine. It can only be done at her pace. I never thought to get into alcoholism and drugs....but it seems that most prostitutes and street people need to deal with the devastating illness of "addiction" in all its forms. I know little or nothing about it all. It is discouraging and it makes me feel helpless and frustrated. It makes me question, yet again, whether I made a mistake, whether all this is not too much for me - more than I expected or am qualified to deal with. It is obvious that I will have to go back to learning again. Funny, when preparing people in the VMM who are going to Africa and Papua New Guinea, we always tell them that the first six months are just to listen and watch. Then, the second six months are there to ask questions, and only after a year do we know how to begin looking for answers. I have reached now the questioning time. For instance: what kind of skills are needed to be of real service to the women?

MINISTRY

There are no supports,
And little concrete, ongoing affirmation.
I have to be convinced,
I cannot expect the conviction to come from
Teddy Bear, or Gypsy, or Stella.
It has to be enough
that I see them smile - or clean
- or happy - or hopeful.
What is wrong with me
That I want to see results and transformations?
When will I be God-centered enough
to leave the harvest to God?
In this ministry, one has to be
totally dependent on God;
leave all results or no-results to God
accept reality exactly how it is,
whilst being fully, and lovingly present

to the people and the situation.
One has no control,
no power,
no plans....no, not even one plan.

5th July, 1983

GOD'S MINISTRY

In all this mess,
In all the pain,
In all the brokenness,
Will I just sit
And murmur,
I am here?
What does it mean,
To be here?
This ministry is new,
Bewildering, confusing,
There are no rules, no guidelines,
No guides,
There are no books,
No maps, no workshops.
Ah - only the Spirit of Jesus
Sitting in the alley.
Only the Grace of God
Hovering in the brothel.
Only the Word of God
Silent, in the scream
Of the siren,
And the shouts
Of drunken men.
Ah - this ministry is surely
Only God's.

6th July, 1983.

I am taking a few days in Wisconsin. Yes - it is good to be here - relaxing and praying. I have only just realised how constantly Teddy has been with me for four months, and how that has taken energy from me, because I have been so concerned and felt so responsible for Teddy. It is important to step back, especially for me, to spend some time alone so that I can get things in perspective. I know it is not good for me to become absorbed by Teddy's needs and growth. I have to find a better balance that will give both of us more space and freedom. It is easy to fall into this trap. Teddy is so much in need. In my naivety, I gave her everything and expected too much, too soon. But I think it is still possible to work at more balance and space. Yes - we can do it!

I have learnt yet another lesson. It is also vital that Teddy grows and develops without feeling that it can only happen if I am there. We have to make the transition now. Teddy can walk by herself now. I love her and I will best show my love by helping her walk more, without me. She will not become strong if I always carry her. These few days of sun and play and beauty help me to breathe deeply. They remind me that all is God's and all belongs to God. Nothing is mine, and nothing and no one should depend on me, but on God alone. God is sufficient! Can I help Teddy to understand that? Can I show her how we have fallen into an addictive pattern of manipulation where I have allowed her and me to think I can be her savior? Every time she is in need she calls me or the community to save her and we jump at it. She needs to learn to take responsibility for herself....she needs to want to do it badly enough. she hasn't a lot of extra time.

Teddy Bear: 9th July, 1983.

Younger Childhood:

As I remember, I wasn't happy. Or not loved. I was like a prisoner at home. My mother did not love me. She never told me that she even cared. When I was very young, maybe 9 or 10, I remember she never let me go out to play. She left me alone in a room while she was away.

I never could leave the room until she let me out to eat or go to school. Never would she talk to me or kiss me, no response of love. It kept on till I was 13. So I said if she don't care, I don't either, so I ran away from home. I didn't want to live at home. I would sleep at friends or on the train track. She couldn't keep me at home, or control me. So I went to the Home where she put me.

The Boarding School: 13-17 years old.

Then I told my caseworker. I don't want to go back home. I said there's no home, or family for me. So then from that day I was awarded to the State (ed. a ward of the State). I went to boarding school. There I was shy. Never opened to anyone, but was always aware of what happened when I was home. I had everything I wanted except love. I found no love. There were house mothers and other girls there. I got along with them very well. I got close to a few of them until one day I ran away. Seeking to find something else. What? I don't know. I was always in trouble. I was impossible. They couldn't control me. I wanted out, so I said, "I'm going away."

I went to California, hitch-hiking. I was fifteen and a half. I got caught and the police shipped me back to the boarding school. I took an overdose of pills. They took me to a hospital for psychiatric help. For twenty one days.

On my seventeenth birthday, I told them I wanted out. Leave me alone. I can do anything I want. I'm grown. So they put me on my own. I was living in one room at the Y.W.C.A. I was still taking pills. Them pills were no good any more, so I went on to the hard stuff. I got addicted. I was 18 then. The little money I got from the State went to my habit.

Drugs and Prostitution: 19 years old.

This was the hardest time of my life. I had such a habit, there wasn't anything for me to do but get out on the street and turn tricks, to support my habit. This went on for a year every night....I was turning tricks with different men. The money went to dope, every last cent. When I was twenty, I met a man (a pimp). I feel in love with him when I thought he felt the same. I really didn't love him, deep inside I didn't. He gave me dope all the time. So I started working for him. I did everything for him. I sold dope for him. I sold my body for him. Did anything he told me to. This went on for three and a half years, till I said I have to get away. I went to New York. I was in a big city all alone. I was still on dope, I started to get withdrawals. I had a bad heroin habit. I remember my first date in that new city. I was scared. Because I heard so much bad things in New York. When I made my first sixty dollars, I found the dope man (naturally!). After three weeks, I wanted to go back to Chicago.

When I got back, I was 22 yrs. old. I got on a drug methadone program for one year. Meantime I was still prostituting. I got pregnant, the baby was premature and had a habit. He lived for only six hours. Months later I got pregnant again. The baby had a habit also and premature. I took him home after one month. I couldn't take care of him. I was supporting my habit and turning tricks. I got him taken away. Mother found me and took him from me. She adopted him when he was two months old. I didn't care. But it hurt. I couldn't take care of him. Life was very hard for me. Why couldn't I just die? My life was ruined. Every day was a nightmare. I was depressed. Hurt. Angry. Confused. Alone. And unloved. Then I was 25. I started drinking in bars. Drinking made me feel better and happy or so I thought, till I started drinking on the streets. Nor did I take care of myself, had no showers, didn't eat well and slept outside on the street.

25-28 years old: Alcoholism and Shelter - Hospital.

The drugs were gone. But the drinking was there. I drank every day till I passed out, I slept in hallways, cars and parks. Winter time, I slept in the shelter at night. Couldn't wait for summer. In the mornings, I was sick. I needed that drink. I got the money from panhandling. Sometimes I would turn a cheap trick for 10-15 dollars. I had no home. I was homeless. Sometimes, I would go to Detox to rest for a day or two. Two years went by. Nothing but drinking and drinking. Not eating. Couldn't eat. I went to the hospital. I had hepatitis and gall stones. So I had my gall bladder taken out. I got released after a month. I stayed off the drink for two days. I started again. I know I was wrong. I didn't care. After six months I was back in hospital again. Hepatitis and now I had sirrhosis. Another operation. I had a shunt put in me. I almost died. The doctor thought I wasn't gonna make it. After three months I got released. I had only two years to live. I said I don't care. I was sick and still drinking.

As you know I ended up back in hospital. That's when I met Edwina. She came to visit me. I had seen her before but I wasn't sober or in the right mind. Since that day I met Edwina, my whole life has changed. I got released. I remember meeting her a couple of times after. I got to know her more. I have only drank, or got drunk twice. She took me off the streets. She offered me a room at the community center.

I told her about myself. At first I didn't tell her I was a prostitute. Gradually I told her. Now we work in street ministry. Now I have found God. My health is getting better. I take care of myself. I pray to God every day. Now Edwina and I are praying for our house. God has helped me in a very special, special way. God helped me through all the pain and suffering that I went through in my life. Edwina has shown me a lot and taught me a lot. She helped me find God. She came a long way to find me, and for me to find Edwina. I am so happy. I have all the love that anybody can ask for. The VMM are my best hope. They taught me to love. They are love. They're very special to me. I love myself.

God is so wonderful.

Teddy.

10th July, 1983.

I am still uneasy about how to work with Teddy. Everything has come at once for her - she wants to be a child, adolescent, adult all at the same time. It is hard to know what to do with all that. I don't know why God has landed me here - when most of the time, if not all the time, I feel totally inadequate for the task at hand. Well - God's grace -

see what you can do with Teddy! I need to be able to cultivate much more patience. I need to really just let God get on with it all.

Teddy Bear: 16th July, 1983.

I've been acting like a six year old these passed few days. I feel very bad about it. I have no reason to act like that because I know there's a lot of people who love me and care for me. But I have been feeling a little down lately. I don't know what it could be.

There is a lot of confusion in me, also anger, stress and tension, that's building and building inside me, that hurts so much. I hope one day that it will all come out and I hope the right way not the wrong way. There's something missing in my life. I can feel it. I wonder what it could be. It's like a small portion missing. Is this all a dream and will I wake up and all of this will be gone? Am I really worth it? Am I something? Or am I just another by-stander?

Teddy.

17th July, 1983.

Gerry killed Carol on 5th July. He was the wino she hung around with. They sort of cared about one another in between being drunk. "Carol, I'm sorry, so sorry, that we could not do anymore for you." I think I understand Gerry's torment more than anyone else. I sat with him on the sidewalk, listening to his loneliness and fears many nights. I don't think Gerry cried with anyone else.

18th July, 1983.

I went to May's. Talked to Howard, Catherine and Belinda. Poor Belinda - not yet twenty and has worked on the streets since she was thirteen. The more I experience these streets and the world of prostitution and drugs, the more I am coming to realise that prostitution just doesn't happen in a vacuum. Statistics citing child incest and child abuse as a pre-condition to a lifestyle of prostitution range from 75% to 94%. What the figures are telling us, in fact, is that for the vast majority of women out on the streets and in the bars touting their bodies, there is an equal number of men - fathers, stepfathers, uncles, grandfathers etc. who first introduced the women to abuse and violence during childhood years. The terrible thing is that society does not go back to the "original sin" and try to understand. Why prostitution? Society compounds the women's sufferings by further punishing them for acting out the consequences of incest and child abuse. Our jails are full of prostitutes (30% of all female inmates are in jail for prostitution). It seems to me our taxes would be put to better use in combatting rapists, child incest abusers, physical abusers and muggers rather than in pursuing prostitutes down side streets. It is a fact that there are more arrests for prostitution in the U.S. than for any other "crime". To take one woman off the streets for a few hours takes a police officer off the street (for reports, court appearances etc.) for the equivalent of nearly three working days. In the meantime, one in four North American women are raped! Why are we so blind? And why are we so slow to understand?

20th July, 1983.

In the evening I took Judy, a friend of mine from school, to the streets and we met Irene. Poor Irene was on the streets with her man - Johnny - trying to get some dates. But she looked so bad - her hair all over the place, her bruised face without make-up - she couldn't get any guys. She was so pleased to see me and I felt deeply sad for her. We took her back to her dingy apartment. There she did her make-up and fixed her hair so she looked really nice. She was transformed and began to feel good about herself. Then we all went out and left her on the streets. I told her I would pray for her. I hope Irene knows she is loved - and perhaps, therefore, she might even feel she is lovable.

21st July, 1983

I received a letter from a woman in jail:

Dear Edwina,

My name is Tracy Jones. I'm an unhappy prostitute of eight years. I have three beautiful children whom I've been blessed to have and I'm now ten weeks pregnant again and it has left me in a deep depression whereas I don't wanna live anymore. I'm just tired and used up. I can't seem to get a start anywhere, but today someone told me about you and that gave me hope for a new life. If I fail this time then I shall kill myself.

I can't believe there is someone who really understands. See, I am very weak and I thought I was alone. See, my hooker friends never discuss the reality of working the streets. All we do is lie to each other. I truly have grown to hate the life. I'm so ashamed of what I am and I do wanna change. I have to. If I don't, I don't wanna live and I'm not bluffing.

When I first started to work the streets my eleven month old girl was murdered by my pimp and this started me to using drugs so I wouldn't have to face the reality of what happened. It got to the point where drugs didn't help me anymore so I joined a drug program. Sure it helped me kick drugs but all of a sudden I was awake and can see what I have become....which is nothing, the scum of the earth.

I have a new little girl. She's eight months old. I love her more than life itself. My father has her and my other two sons. She's what made me wanna change in the first place. It's just that I have no place to start. I still work the streets for bus fare and food and rent money. So how can I stop? When will I ever have the chance to raise my children when I can't get started? See, by me always being high while I was working - it's hard to turn a trick in the right state of mind - that's what's killing me. But I can't survive.

I know no other way but the streets. I tried a shelter and at 6.00 a.m they woke me and said I had to leave. That discouraged me and I turned tricks to pay for my room every day. You know what we learned about the street life is that no one can change unless they are truly fed up. You can't do it for your kids, or for your parents, but for yourself.

What I am asking for is a new life and I can't make it without the help of someone who knows exactly what I'm going through. See, I'm sick in the mind and I hurt just thinking of what I've been through. Now I'm doing seventy days in the Cook County jail for stealing clothes for my kids and myself. I should be getting out next month and I'll be about four months pregnant then and I don't wanna go back to abusing myself. So I am going to need a place to stay temporary and someone to show me how to get on Public Aid. I don't have a social security card and that's gonna take time. In the meanwhile, I don't wanna turn tricks to survive.

I'm willing to work, scrub floors, and things just for your ear to listen and guide me and a place to lay my head. Without your help I don't think I can make it. I'll sleep on the floor.

See, I believe in God and Jesus Christ and if it wasn't for him spurring me on, one of my tricks would have killed me by now. I believe I'll be forgiven for my sins, but if I kill myself, then I'll never see my little girl in Heaven. Please, please, please help me so I can help myself. You are a blessing to hookers. I didn't think anyone cared, and even if you don't help me, just continue your good work. If you change or turn a few people in the right direction then your work is not in vain.

Prostitution isn't related to anything else. It is a sickness of its own, like cancer. Cancer is the root of the problem and it's the same with real hookers. We are a desperate kind of people, and prostitution is the root of our problem.

Please guide me. I'm not asking for charity. I'm willing to work for a bed to sleep in, temporarily, while I get Public Aid together. Please don't turn your back.

Thank you.

Tracy Jones.

We have to find a house!

22nd July, 1983.

THE PEROXIDE HOOKER

Down the alley
The peroxide hooker
Dove furtively in search
Of a quick job
For five bucks.
(Used to be ten -
But times are hard
And we cannot be choosey.)
The decoy cop cruised up
And beckoned to
The peroxide hooker,
To hassle for the price
And the service to be given...
She shot for ten and then
In desperation....five.
The badge was flashed
And spitting and snarling,
To bite back tears,
The peroxide hooker was
Bundled in the back seat
And sped triumphantly
To the big red jail
We built for her.
We put prison bars around her,
And high tiled walls,
So we would not see
The peroxide hooker cry
And spit on us
In grief turned to fury
And pain turned to hate.
We nailed her to our public cross

And, shaking our heads,
Tutting her sin,
We left the hooker
To die alone
In the shame
She was born in.
We turned away
From the peroxide hooker
And fled to the dark safety
Of the sacred church walls
To pray for God's mercy
For the woman on the cross.
To pray for God's mercy
For the woman on the cross.

23rd July, 1983.

This is a good day for me, one of prayer and quiet. I am coming to realise more and more, how much I need to spend time alone. I have been close to despair because I have not given myself any space or silence. I know I cannot be involved in this ministry without that.

Teddy has been difficult lately - moody and childish. This has been a cause of anger and frustration in me. I can only deal with it if I am at peace within and can draw, therefore, on inner sources. I must continually nurture myself, giving myself quiet and solitude to be alone with God. I have to remember that nothing depends on me - only on God. My relationship with God must be a priority if anything good and positive is to come out of any other relationship.

I want to help Teddy to grow and be independent - it demands much more understanding and tolerance and patience than I have ever been able to show. How can I walk with a precious person who, out of her addiction, keeps choosing a self-destructive path!

I walked the streets alone in the evening. It is strange to walk alone. I realise how long it is since I met Teddy, and walked with her for the first time. I remember the lonely days and nights I spent on the streets knowing no one. I was often afraid, I still am! I still feel very vulnerable being alone in this area of the city.

I talked for a while to Virginia who sits on the steps of the Church and works the streets around. She has great fantasies about her past as a sophisticated call girl, dancer, and delights in telling them. Behind her stories I can hear her heart-scream, telling me she has been badly hurt and is a lonely and frightened woman. There is much that she could teach me if ever she was willing to tell me her history. Tonight, Irene called from Wisconsin, with a stolen credit card. She wanted to tell me she has left Chicago. I fear for her. Unless she stops running and gets help she will keep going down fast. But I am glad and encouraged that she called. I have become, maybe, a point of reference for her. That may be all I can be for her now.

24th July, 1983.

Went to visit Gerry in jail. He's doing okay. His court hearing is Friday. He says he did not kill Carol, that he only hit her in the face. Who knows what the truth is? Both their lives were already a witness to death. I came home very tired. Teddy had gone off again. I'm trying not to worry about her. I hope I can sleep. Will we start all over again? It will be a miracle if she is not drinking again. Sometimes I wonder how I will survive, and how I will continue to hope and believe. I want so much for the miracle of life to become manifested in Teddy - but who am I to know what the miracle should look like?

Please God.....

25th July, 1983.

Teddy has not come in. She has been out all day and night. I feel very helpless and distressed. She needs her freedom and must have it to make whatever choices she has to make. I have to learn that even if people want to hurt themselves they must be free to do so. But it is so hard to stand and watch and wait. Must I watch her die? It is lonely and agonising. I love Teddy dearly and have watched her sparkle and grow. I do not want to see her die again. I question my ethical stance. Surely if I see someone about to jump off a bridge, I would do what I could to stop the madness. I wouldn't stand and watch the person die. Is it the urgency of death that makes the difference? Does the timing involved in the dying make it imperative that I stand by?

I have no control over Teddy's urge for freedom - even if it is destructive. I have tried to do what I thought was good for her, to divert her from her path. Maybe I have failed. I do not know that I could do anything else but stand by. I know I hurt a lot and am very fearful for her. I pray that God, who brought her into my life, will take care of her and let her live and grow through all this. Maybe she will stay out all night again. I am trying to pray for confidence and faith! I pray - please God, take care of her.

HOPE

Even at the gates of hell,
Believe in redemption.
Let my grace and power work,
Where you have none.
It is only for you
To believe and to trust.
Be confident.
Trust.
Love.
Do not condemn.
Believe,
In the face of unbelief.
Hope against hope.
This is faith.
This is the gift most needed
For those who have suffered
So deeply, and lost all.
You must manifest love and hope.
It is only then
That my people will begin to
Believe in themselves.

26th July, 1983.

Teddy hasn't shown up yet. If I only knew she was okay, I would be alright. But I feel so helpless. It is this not knowing which is so hard, Lord. Yes - this ministry is hard. There may never be any tangible fruits. I might never be able to tell your miracles apart. There is a lot of hurt and pain here where you have called me. I have ended up by sharing, not only my faith, but their hurt and their pain. I am learning what it is to be afraid, and insecure, and alone.

It is now 8.00 p.m. - Teddy called from New York! She just jumped on a bus and off she went. She says she is prepared to come back and start again. Yes, we could start again!

Please Lord, guide me and help me to be patient and understanding.

It is now midnight - I talked to Teddy in New York. She sounded afraid, tired and lonely. She is a child in a jungle. She doesn't know her bearings - not that she doesn't know right from wrong. She does! She needs to choose freely in life - but how free can she be with such a burden of inflicted pain crushing her?

THE MIRACLE

The miracle is not forgiveness of sins,
The miracle is our believing love.
May we see wonders -
The wonders of ourselves
As we become aware of God's
Great love - God's light.
Throwing our sins to the bottom of the sea
Removing them as far as East from West
Redeeming our life from the grave.
We often think we are dying -
We are worth little....
God wants to throw all our sin
Into the depths of the sea

And raise us from the pits.
What holds us back is our
Disbelief in such love,
God's waiting, longing
Anticipating love
Expectant....
We must rise from the grave
By believing in God's crazy love.
Only God could love so passionately.
As long as we believe that
We belong in the pit and in the grave,
As long as we believe
We are less than
The beautiful and beloved children
Of God,
There will be no miracles.

The darkness I have been in these last few days cost me a lot. I believe God has been with me through it all, gently leading me through my weakness and blindness, leading Teddy through hers. There will be new life. But - Oh - the death that comes first!

27th July, 1983.

Teddy came back! She is confused and, I think, afraid. Although she tries hard not to show it, she comes across as aggressive and difficult. She spent all the money she had, and drank, shot drugs, and who knows what else. I know now how stressed I was, by my relief to see her back. I still believe she can make it. It has been a hard and painful learning experience for me. I have to stop looking for the big miracles, and to stop looking for someone or something to blame when they do not come about. It is the little miracles - not so little when I begin to add them up - that show me how to believe in the goodness of people, that help me to hope when society claims one more failure, one more death.

I am trying to get Stella on Welfare and Disability. It is another struggle. She is terrified at the questions and the interviews - she thinks someone is going to "get her". Maria and I managed to piece together some of her story. It seems she lived with her brothers who got in trouble with the law and who one day just abandoned her. She stayed in the house, not daring to go out, waiting for them to come back, or at least to get in touch. Finally hunger forced her out, but, afraid the police would come and take her away, she never went back to the house. For the last seven years she has been hiding in the streets. I have to explain to her that no one is going to take her away; coax her into telling enough of her story so we can get the documents we need; and reassure her that we will not abandon her like her brothers did. She is so afraid.

Dear Lord - your people are afraid and lonely. Help me not to catch the disease of fear but always, even whilst surrounded by fear and misery, to be a sign of hope and confidence. Let my life bring a little joy into all this despair.

Teddy Bear: 27th July, 1983.

I'm back. I feel really bad. Why did I do it? I'm losing my mind. I did it again, ran away from nothing. No reason. I hurt so many people that I love. I should leave. I don't deserve this at all. They don't deserve it at all. I will go away. "Oh God, please help me." (Confused.) Teddy Bear.

28th July, 1983.

Spent six hours in Social Security and Public Aid getting Stella's papers through. It is a demeaning experience to be in the midst of such humiliation and human sadness. These people are at the bottom of the heap. I got Stella through, however, and now she will have food stamps and an income. It is the first big step towards getting a place of her own.

I feel a sadness - a depression within me. I am aware that my sparkle and joy are gone and this concerns me. Teddy and all the anxiety and energy her last running-away cost me, must be contributing to this depression. Also, my concern for Stella, the lack of supportive community life, and my failure to maintain a constant prayer life are factors that need to be considered. I am tempted to blame the ministry, to suggest that this is not the kind of work I should be doing, to want to run it down, and to find something else less taxing and draining, but, it is just a temptation! It does not come from God. God does not play games! God does not do sudden and traumatic "about-turns". Is it that I do not rely enough on God? God, God alone .....God is the only one who can sustain me in all this. All else is peripheral! Have I made all else central, and God peripheral? If I lack private time, being with God in silent listening, I will lack peace and confidence. Faith is not enough! I need to find the holy space, the sacred time here in the city, in the midst of the noise, the smell, the pollution, the poverty, and the violence. I need to transport an imaginary, yet real, forest and birds and hermitage to the streets in Chicago, where I can be alone with God, to experience God as my lover. I need to do this for myself, for the women who have no access to the beauty of Creation, for other ministers who may come after me and who may get exhausted much too soon otherwise.

I am doing "good deeds". It is acceptable to God but it is not enough! No action nor even a thousand good deeds can make up for the lack of prayer. How, in this crazy, erratic ministry am I going to find the discipline to pray constantly? I don't want to become a burnt out, lukewarm disciple of Jesus. I have to be alive and sparkling, because the Good News of God is alive and sparkling. If I am "dead" and depressed I am giving a different message - the message of oppression and hopelessness that the women in the streets hear all the time.

11.00 p.m.....Teddy was out. I drove to look for her and found her drunk on the streets. I told her I loved her and asked her to come home. But she would not. She began to cry and told me to please leave her alone. So I did and came back. Once again, I am deeply sad. Helpless! Only God!

Teddy called at 1.00 a.m. - drunk and crying.

29th July, 1983.

I phoned Maria and Su to tell them about Teddy. Maria and Su, are my good friends, they are my community, my family, who have supported me in all of this. Maria joined me after I started VMM, the Volunteer Missionary Movement in England, and we have been together since then. It has been almost ten years. She is a Cuban woman, strong and loyal. She gives a lot of time to listening to the women when they need to talk or cry. Su, a Yorkshire woman, joined us later and for some years the three of us have formed community. Su was one of my main supports during my time in the Trailer and during this year on the streets. The women like Su because of her laughter and infectious sense of humor. It would be hard to without the haven of the home and forest provided by Su and the VMM Community. The little community there welcomes every street person, every prostitute I bring with open arms. They help me provide an experience of family and love and care that otherwise would not be possible. I feel lucky to have these two sisters of mine at my side. They worry about me and with me - they love me and they love Gypsy and Joe and Stella and Teddy and all the others.

30th July, 1983.

I drove to May's and spent a few hours there. Catherine, Carol and Belinda (the dancer) were there. I still ask myself a lot of questions as to my role in such a place. Then I drove back and found Teddy drunk on the streets again. She ran off down the street screaming and shouting abuse at me. It was so hard to take. I felt such a heavy pain inside myself! It was also hard to get in the car and drive away, but I knew it was the best thing to do. Gypsy was with me and I felt comforted by his presence. I am so tired. I don't know how or why I still believe she can make it, but I do. I am trying to understand who I should be - what I need to be for Teddy, for all the other women on the streets. I search for God in all this. I feel very lonely and alone.

I believe. I trust. I feel alone. My mind keeps going round and round searching for a fragment of truth that will allow all the little pieces to fall into place, but truth escapes me at this time. I can only feel the pain, and cannot think of a good reason for the pain, nor can I see any way out of this constant battering of my senses. I do not understand. But I trust. I keep repeating this like a litany. I trust. If I say it often enough, maybe I will relax and trust. I pray for Teddy. Her life is very important. All the lives of the women I have met are so, so important. God knows it - I know it - why can't they?

31st July, 1983.

Today was Sunday and it was a truly blessed day for me. I have felt so free and relaxed and aware of God's love and presence in me today. It is a joyous and peace-filled experience after all the tensions and trauma of this past week. I am so grateful to God for this time of renewal.

I spent the evening walking with Gypsy and met a variety of people. I talked for a while to Chris, a prostitute, who comes from a little town in Wisconsin. We sat in Pigeon Square. Here, in this little space where four roads meet, I can meet the pimps, the prostitutes, the "bag ladies", the winos, the johns and even at times, other ministers who work in the area. Strangers pass by in their big cars, not aware of how much life there is in this small concrete space. Chris shoots drugs and tonight she was very weepy and depressed. She says she wants to quit it all, but somehow can't take that step.

There is much pain, but I must learn to be patient:

> The seed grows and bears fruit not
> because of our talents and gifts
> but because we leave space in
> our darkness for God to take root.

Teddy Bear: 31st July, 1983,.

I thank God for not letting me die. One day I will understand myself more clearly. Sometimes I wonder about myself. Will I survive this terrible pain that I'm doing to myself? Will I wake up one day? The truth is, I think, I'm scared. I am afraid! Sometimes I wish I can start all over again, and live over again. I also wish that this community never knew that I exist. Do I really wish this? (No).

Teddy Bear: 2nd August, 1983.

Dear Dolores,
Please let me know why you won't help me find you. Why are you so scared of letting me know? I think I know how you feel. Because I feel the same way sometimes. But we can't get along with each other, or anyone else if we can't find each other. One day we will get together and talk about each other's situations so you can help me and I will help you. We both are the same in some way. We will get together, we will spend a little time alone. A quiet place. With nobody but Teddy and Dolores, O.K.? Love you.

      Teddy Bear.

I just wrote to Dolores. I think she feels better because I do. Thank you God!

Teddy Bear: 7th August, 1983.

Lord,
I pray for Eskimo Joe. Please let him be happy and well. I miss him so much. Let him be safe wherever he is. We know he sleeps on the streets. I love him so much. He is my brother. The brother I never had. You know and I know that deep down he is not happy. So please stay with Joe. Guide Joe. Please show Joe happiness and laughter. I hope I see Joe this week. So many loved ones that he really cared for, left Joe or died. One day Joe will have a home of Joe's. His, not anybody else's.

Lord,
I pray also for my son that he is in good health and safe. I do worry of him at times and I do think of him at times. And love him at certain times of my life. Sometimes I wonder what he is doing or even what he looks like. I did not see him while he was growing - out of baby time. He is five years and three months now. Lord I know I can not have him as my son, but please, watch Alan. Let him not walk in my terrible steps. Let him see life the right way. Not the way I did. He will be somebody one day. Not like me, a nobody, a nothing. Take care of Alan. Let him be free. Let him seek wisdom. Lord. Is Alan blooming? Will Alan ever know who I am?
A lonely, confused,

Love, Teddy Bear.

The evening was happy. We all saw a good film together. I feel more at ease now. Another night. All alone in a quiet lonesome room. I don't know why I feel this way. But I rather be alone. I guess it's because I never had PRIVACY before. This is the first time in my life I can remember privacy. That could be it, anyways, I feel sleepy. Thank you Lord for another day.

Teddy.

7th August, 1983. Yorkville.

IN THE FOREST

I am more and more convinced
that nature reflects the face of God.
There is such a deep profound peace in this forest;
Wild flowers have burst out everywhere
and the song of the birds fills the air;
The breeze carries the sweet smell
of warm rain and spring blossoms;
Everything pulsates with God's life.
She breathes her amazing beauty tenderly,
tenderly, through the moist rich earth.

Early in the morning, the sun comes up and throws warm light on the dew damp grass. The birds go wild with song! Everything smells fresh and pure. I feel like tip-toeing so as not to intrude or disturb in any way.....

God offers a myriad of these creation experiences. Even though we have churned so much of our world up in destruction, there is still beauty available. We can look towards the Universe and see God generously offering us infinite ways to reach harmony. We need eyes to see and heart to think with.

8th August, 1983.

Today there is a dark mood brewing all around me. I talked to Teddy wanting her to understand what I felt. I don't know if she can hear me. Sometimes I feel like giving up. I feel I cannot talk anymore - the wondering, the anxiety, the waking up late at night...hoping to find Teddy safe. I am afraid to find her when she wants to lose herself. Sometimes I am afraid of all the pain and worry. Does she know what it is like to sit at home throughout the night waiting, praying, afraid? Is she dead, sick, drunk, in prison, hurt....? My imagination is fertile during the night of silence.

Something in me whispers - "she doesn't care" .... "Tell her to go to hell so that you might live in peace." Everytime I try again with her I feel weaker than the last time. People have always said I am a strong woman. Sometimes I am tired of being a strong woman. Sometimes this strong woman hurts a lot and wants to go far away. Sometimes I need to receive strength rather than give it. Sometimes I, too, want to run away......

9th August, 1983. Chicago.

Returned from Yorkville yesterday with Teddy and Stella. I visited Laura. She is a working prostitute who was taken more dead than alive to hospital after having been beaten up by her pimp. The hospital called me and I went and talked to her distraught parents. She shows the same pattern as the others - Laura was insecure in childhood and did not feel loved. Her parents love her but their own hurts made it impossible to show love. This is the sin - that we pass on to our children and our children's children - the hurt and the injustices our parents received from their parents. Unless some miracle happens to break the chain, we become victims of those who should love us most.

Teddy disappeared. She went off yesterday afternoon and did not contact me till 7.30 a.m. this morning. I was anxious. I am so tired of all this. Waiting, wondering, afraid....I feel angry. And yet in all my hurt and anger something struggles in me, whispering, "Understand! Forgive! She's sick and afraid." I am struggling to be strong when everything in me is weary of strength. I want to say "ENOUGH" I want to give up. I read some of Teddy's journal:

August 2nd, 1983.

I think I remember a very long time ago asking God to help me, and God has got Edwina for me. I hope she never gives up. I can't never lose her, God. I will try very hard on my behalf. I feel this is the last chance. Oh God, please don't let Edwina give up on me. Not yet please, I need her. She's all I got....

I must not give up, even though I am screaming inside.

Today I went to Church and the first reading must have been chosen by God!

"Be strong, stand firm; you are going with this people into the land which Yahweh swore to their fathers he would give them; you are to give it into their possession. Yahweh himself will lead you; he will be with you; he will not fail you or desert you. Have no fear, do not be disheartened." (Duet. 31: 7-8)

Please God, be my strength. Keep me going, keep me believing that miracles are possible.

10th August, 1983.

Teddy came back after two days drunk. I have to be very careful of letting the pain and anxiety disturb me in the very core of my being. When I am anxious and disturbed I lose touch with my trust and faith. I must do all I can with the women that come into my life, and then let it be with God. I have not yet learnt this deepest trust, the one that lets my guts relax, not needing to name the miracles. Maybe Teddy's miracle will not be the quitting of alcohol, even if I believe she is killing herself. God will take care of Teddy and the street people and the girls in the brothel and I must let God take over. I have no power! I can only trust! I am limited, and cannot change people or control their behavior or make their choices in life. The Compassionate God never gives up on Her people. She is always offering new choices, new alternatives. When we say No to one alternative or fail to choose another, God does not lose heart, but comes up with other possibilities. My ministry is to offer the alternatives that I see and encourage these women to choose one they feel more comfortable with. There are many roads to God - an infinite number really - God doesn't care which one we choose. God allows us more freedom than we can imagine. When the alternatives I offer are not taken up I must not become distraught and anxious. I must let God take over, use the gift of imagination and be thankful that I am given the grace to try again.

For my imagination to soar, to search the infinite mind of God, I must be more open to the Spirit. It is the Spirit who planted the seed in my "womb" so God can be made flesh within me. I must allow God to take over more of my life. Ah - now I feel the need of a hermitage experience! Why was it backwards? How can I relive it here in the streets? My spirituality was born out of contradictions and chaos, and it is there that it is constantly renewed.

Teddy Bear: 10th August, 1983.

> I feel terrible
> I feel like a jerk.
> I'm very sorry.
> Teddy.

14th August, 1983.

I am sitting outside the hermitage in Yorkville. The community is there, always ready to welcome me, to try to understand. They are worried about me, and about how I am getting so tired. I try to pretend, but they see through me. Now, however, I am alone. Oh, it is so beautiful! I am surrounded by trees and wild flowers. I can hear the birds and the crickets. This is a haven of peace and joy - a little Eden where I can feel strength and peace flowing back into me. This place is a special gift from God who, in great wisdom, knew how much I would need it.

It has been a hard time with Teddy. I have given her an ultimatum - to see an alcoholic counsellor on a regular basis. She has agreed and we will go together on Tuesday. But if it does not work I will have absorbed a great learning experience. The ultimate freedom is that which allows a person to be who she wishes to be. Freedom is real when the choice is made with a clear awareness of all other options, and the person is of a sane mind. I have given Teddy that option. I must accept her choice.

Teddy Bear: 15th August, 1983.

I really have to try my best. I will be somebody, and I know it will be pain-ful and hard. It will hurt a lot. I'm really happy that I have someone to be with and stand by me. I won't never be alone. Thank you Lord.

ME AND SEA
(by Teddy Bear)

When I see
I see the sea
The sea is like a deep cool breeze.

When I see me
I hear a seed growing,
growing beautiful by the water.

When I see me
I feel sand,
by the sandy sea.

When I see me
I see God
by the sea.

Me and Sea
Beautiful God.

Teddy Bear: 20th August, 1983.

Dear Lord,

Please help me make the right decision. I want to do what I think is the right thing to do. Help me be mature enough to make it right. So help me be strong. I want to be a strong woman so I can help Edwina do her work. She needs someone to work with and I want to be the one to do so. Please hear me Lord. Thank you.

One day I will be a strong mature woman.

Teddy.

22nd August, 1983.

Teddy is doing well. It was a struggle for her to seek help, but she saw the counsellor and liked him. It is our biggest breakthrough. Yesterday we both went to our first AA open meeting and it was excellent. A woman spoke about her life for over an hour. It was very powerful. I think even Teddy was impressed. That was breakthrough # 2! And I think breakthrough # 3 is happening today - Teddy has gone off to work as a day-laborer. That means a day's work with pay - I feel both cautious and hopeful.

I feel more lonely than I have ever felt before. The problems are many and deep and the ministers do not abound. The VMM community is supportive and wonderful but I know that in many ways I am alone with Teddy and Laura and Joyce and Gypsy and Stella and the others, until other ministers come to share in this work. God, the gentle minister, I take for granted - I wouldn't be here otherwise. I wonder when God will find a home for us? It could be, maybe, when Teddy is more on her feet. Perhaps God waits for Teddy instead of Teddy waiting for God? I must tell her.

Now, I am getting more involved with Laura and I wonder what she needs to do to save her life. Would offering her a house make a difference to the choices she needs to make? I wonder. More and more I believe that they need to belong to someone, to a place, to a dream.

I received $375.00 for talks I gave recently. This side of my work is growing at the present time and I am grateful for it. It is my only source of income apart from the little whorehouse. God provides! I feel for the first time in a while, a real hope that something very good and positive is happening. A foundation is being laid.

10.00 p.m. Well, I'm glad I wrote that I was cautiously hopeful - Teddy hasn't come back yet! She is obviously out drinking the money she earned today. Today, I also spent five hours sitting with Stella at the doctor's. I spend long hours wondering how much of this ministry is simply sitting, waiting, hoping. It is a ministry of the powerless, only demanding presence and invitation, which mostly becomes invitation refused!

I have done all I can for Teddy. When she chooses to drink I can only stand by. I don't give up, but my role is one of silently waiting and hoping.

I feel the pain of knowing that Teddy is now sick, smelly, ugly and with no control over herself. The pain comes from being in a position to see her other side too - all the beautiful possibilities which are overwhelmed by the ugly reality of the limitations.

This evening I visited Laura in hospital. She is doing well and there seems to be hope. She wants to start a new life. She could make it, and I talk to her about choices she needs to make. I have learnt a lot from my experience with Teddy. I will not allow myself to be swallowed up by others like I am with Teddy sometimes. I will walk with Laura, but I will not walk for Laura. I will love her, but not more than I love myself. I will help her find herself without losing me in the process. She has a responsibility for her own life that she needs to claim. I felt alone tonight and wished I had someone to go out to dinner with. I had planned to take Teddy out as a surprise.

23rd August, 1983.

Teddy is still gone. She came back late - slept a few hours and was gone again when I returned at 9.45 a.m., from visiting Laura in hospital. For all my efforts at detachment and self-control, I feel worried about Teddy. I have prayed all day that God takes care of her.

Dear God - why don't you give me a break?

It is tempting to think I've messed things up, but I will not give into that. I am no saint, but I TRY. Why, God, why? And how am I going to cope with inspiring others when I can hardly get myself together?

Dear God - don't push me too hard.....

Take care of Teddy. Take care of me.

> Help me to keep going
> keep believing
> keep hoping
> Help me to keep believing
> in miracles
> Roses on the Broadway

I am deeply sad. I am struggling just to hold onto this crazy dream, this dark and lonely ministry. Oh, yes, it is dark alright!

27th August, 1983.

Teddy called this morning - drunk and helpless!

It was a great relief just to know she's alive, but at the same time I know, because of this repeated pain and disappointment, that there is a degree of restraint and detachment entering into my relationship with Teddy. It is the only way I can remain sane and healthy. Where do Teddy and I go from here? I do not know. Are we to go from drunken binge to drunken binge? Whatever she chooses to do, she chooses, but do I have to stay and watch her die?

I pray constantly that she will be healed. All I can do is pray for her, and carry on living my own life as normally as possible. I pray that God will touch her, hold her, heal her...

28th August, 1983.

I visited Laura in hospital and on the way saw Teddy. She saw me too. She was drunk but walking steadily enough. At first she smiled and began walking towards the car. But, suddenly she stopped and turned away. She walked off into the park and never looked back.

10th September, 1983.

Teddy applied and has been accepted into a residential treatment program. Ah! A breakthrough! Will she make it? Will she hold out? To symbolise a new beginning, Teddy dropped her street name and claimed her real baptismal name - Dolores. She said it was time for her real self to break through! This is my greatest hope! Seven months of hoping, failing, pain, disappointment..... I think now - she is going to really make it. She actually insists on being called Dolores, instead of Teddy Bear. A turn-around! I am so relieved. How did I survive? This is surely the new beginning, the new Jerusalem for Dolores. What a painful journey, God. Will they all be like that?

Tonight, I spent the evening with a Canadian friend, Ted Wood. Ted is a young man, quiet and gentle. He has a vision of a world where all are equal and he wants to be part of building it. We discussed the problems and advantages of having a man share this ministry. The obvious disadvantage is that he represents the males that have oppressed these women, the fathers and uncles that raped them, the pimps that abuse them, the clients or johns that use them, the judges and police that persecute them and punish them. The advantage, if Ted is sufficiently mature to handle it, is that the women have an opportunity ot have a healthy relationship with a man - maybe for the first time in their lives. Ted is going to join me - to share in renting a house and start a ministerial community in January. I am very happy to have a peer and companion. Another breakthrough! God is at work. Ah - what next?

Dolores: 1st September, 1983.

Dear God,
I love myself for what I'm gonna be some day. I will be someone, some-body soon. When I get strong. I love you.

Dolores: 6th September, 1983.

I'm looking forward to going into this treatment program. I'm so proud
of myself. I know it will be a success for me. I can feel it. I know
God must be looking down on me, smiling.

Dolores.

13th September, 1983.

Yet another full day! I took Stella to a residential home for the elderly.
I'm sure it's the best place for her. Well, she is going Thursday for a
two week trial - another blessing! Her money from Social Security is
not enough but a parish in the suburbs has agreed to cover the
difference. What would she do otherwise? Go back to the streets?
Within two weeks, both Dolores and Stella are beginning new lives! I
feel like a child on her birthday. So many gifts! A time for blessings
has come! Will the house be next? Dolores is doing well in the
program and is learning a lot. I hope she may be different when she
gets back. Everything is in flux at present, but even in this joy I must
continue letting God be. But it is good, and I can't help feeling high,
that maybe, after all, there will be results for all to see!

There is a new creation; an intensity of "coming about". God is at
work and I am in awe. God is smiling. There is a new birth and I am
deeply grateful. There is a young rose growing on the Broadway. I
hear the seed growing.

16th September, 1983.

STANLEY

The police shot Stanley today -
in self defence they said.
I remember Stanley well -
A young effeminate man,

who wore floral shirts
and tight cut-off jeans.
He was a male prostitute,
a gentle, hurting man,
looking for love,
down the back alleys.
Stanley's eyes used to light up
when we met
at the busy intersection.
He would fling his arms around me
and tell me I was beautiful.
He would do a little dance of joy,
when I told him,
he, too, was beautiful.
Stanley never did fit into
this harsh and violent world.
His floral shirt and cheap bracelets
were incongruous
amidst the garbage and rage
of the streets where he wandered.
Stanley, elegant, beautiful,
and so, so alone,
lying in a pool of blood.
Three bullets through his smooth chest.
I think, had I been there
before the pistols fired,
Stanley would have clasped his arms around me
sobbing, sobbing.
There would have been a flood of tears,
instead of a pool of blood.

Dolores: 17th September, 1983.

Oh Lord! I'm so hurt inside. So lonely. It hurts so much. But I'm happy. I know I'm doing the best, being here. I want to be with Edwina. It's only 20 more days. Please help me from the loneliness and pain.

Dolores.

20th September, 1983.

This feels like a sacred moment....it seems a long time since I have stopped and felt and been alone. Breaking this new ground is lonely and I still do not know where we will live. I think God is going to leave it right up to the last minute, like God always does, or maybe I will have to wait beyond the last minute. I am surely ready now for a place I can call home!

Dolores: 22nd September, 1983.

I am beautiful and also friendly and charming....and a little bit thick headed. I have so much going for me that I never realized before. So many friends. I mean real friends, not artificial. I can be loving and kind. I'm growing to love and be loved. When I get out I'm gonna prove it too. I'm gonna tell the whole world about how beautiful I am and I will be kind and thoughtful to anyone that needs my help. Even to the one that doesn't need my help, I'm gonna prove what God is telling me to say and do. I never understand myself, for the reason I never gave myself a chance and didn't care, but now I do care. I understand very well. I also understand I should make decisions about my life, because it's not really that difficult. I must fight this race like Edwina says, "Fight, you can do it!" And I will. It's hard but I will do it. Fight, fight and I will win.

Dolores: 23rd September, 1983.

I'm trying to forget my pain. It hurts so much. It not easy. Sometimes I cry. I cried a lot today. I'm trying to be happy. I feel bad for many reasons. I have never been through anything like this. Specially feeling alone.

Loneliness can be frightening and it hurts. Hurts in a way that makes you sick and tense. It feel like the lake when a storm appears and the waves are very strong and the high waves hit against big rocks. My nerves feel like fire works on the 4th July.

Dolores.

23rd September, 1983.

These last few days have been very full. I have spent a couple of hours with Irene trying to help her decide to go for alcoholic treatment. She is very sick but won't go for treatment. May won't keep her any more so I took her to a transient hotel where she can stay for a while. She still wants to work and denies any problem. Irene is a beautiful person. When sober, she is gentle and kind, with a wit and a sense of humor that can even get the brothel laughing. My taking Irene to the hotel led to a chain of events. I met the manager. He seems like a good man and might prove to be a good contact. A few hours after I met him, he called with news of a runaway teenager from Minneapolis. Before I got to the hotel, the teenager, Jo-Jo, had gone off to the police station with Michelle, a call-girl prostitute who used to work the streets but now "does" conventions in the big hotels. Michelle, seeing Jo-Jo's youth, wants to save her from the lifestyle that she, seasoned prostitute, knows is destructive. She has become protective of Jo-Jo, and anxious to see that she is placed safely in the care of the youth authorities. Ah, these women prostitutes know their pain and the high cost of their lifestyle!

26th September, 1983

Today was a beautiful day with Dolores. She was out on a pass for the day. We talked about her progress and her future. I began to see a new creation - a new life building in her. God has worked wonders. We spent an hour sitting on the sidewalk with Eskimo Joe. He wept and asked me, "Why do you care about people like me and Gypsy?" I was deeply moved but could not answer. The street people are surprised when "straight" people show they really care. They can't understand why anyone should bother.

I look back at my awareness, or lack of it, about street people, the homeless, the poor and realize they really are invisible people. They get relegated to certain parts of town so the "decent folk" don't have to look at them - so we don't have to feel guilty as we consume enough for three, or even ten.

Today, I also had a telephone message from Gypsy - "I am in DeTox as you recommended...." I am unsure, uncertain....will Gypsy make it too? Do mountains move all at once, all at the same time? What can possibly motivate these people into joining the ranks of the stable in our society?

Dolores: 29th September, 1983.

I, myself, Dolores, have learned a lot from my program. My treatment was very good. I learned all about alcoholism. What it does, and how it affected my life. I know now that it is a disease that's uncontrollable and that I'm powerless over alcohol. I also learned about what A.A. is all about and how it works which I never knew before I came here. And also the higher power over all this which is important to me. Also learned to love and understand more. I grew a lot (maturity) also I got to love myself and respect myself and to know ME specially I learned to give and receive. I'm so happy that I did make this choice.

Dolores.

5th October, 1983.

Time is going very fast and there is much to be done before I leave to visit England on 1st November. It will be hard to go now, just when things are beginning to happen and come to fulfillment. The good news is that Catholic Charities gave me $12,000.00 to pay rent for a house for a year. It is a beginning! I have a lot of other places to write to, now that I have a foundation grant. Now, we need the house we can make into a home!

Dolores completes her program tomorrow - a great event. She begins her new life. We will have a welcome dinner for her. She will need a job and this will not be easy with her history, plus the high unemployment in the Uptown area.

7th October, 1983.

It has been a very good day. I am in Yorkville for the weekend and have brought Stella, Mark (Gypsy) and Dolores. It is good for all of us to be here, together, a motley crew sustaining and caring for each other, experiencing community and sharing. I thank God for our diversity and our unity. Tonight we played cards and laughed a lot. I thank God for all the laughter, for bringing such an unlikely group together in such an unlikely place - "bag lady", wino, prostitute, missionaries and ministers here in the middle of the country at the VMM center! I sat back and looked at this group marvelling at God's fertile imagination. Our society praises uniformity while God plays with infinite diversity. Our society insists on conformity while God rejoices in those who dare to dance to a different tune. Our society lauds those who acquire more and more material goods, while God isconstantly giving away all God has and is. Only God would think it just right that we who are so different would meet as equals, journeying together on our unique roads.

8th October, 1983.

I spent the morning on fund-raising - how I hate that! It makes me feel quite dead. Dolores and I spent some time together this afternoon, just fooling around the shopping mall. Dolores treated me to dinner. We talked and I explained to her why I had to go to England...asking for her understanding and support. I am still very much involved in the VMM and carry the responsibility of participating in decision-making and policy procedures. This year, also, I am to visit some of our lay missionaries in Africa and see how they are doing. I am beginning to feel torn between my commitment to work for the VMM and this new ministry here in Chicago. However, my confidence in Dolores and her potential is growing. I think she will be fine without me for a while.

Dolores: 9th October, 1983.

It is so great to be sober. It is like being born all over again. I feel normal again. I can laugh, really laugh and enjoy life. The right way. Not being drunk and unhappy or feeling lonely or depressed. It is like taking a deep breath of fresh air. I love myself also I feel for people like I never had before. I know myself and know who I am. and know what life is all about. All because I am sober and can accept life. Life is what you make of it! And I love and enjoy it, every minute of it.

Dolores: 11th October, 1983.

Maria, Su, Edwina and me went out to dinner. They took me to the most elegant restaurant I ever been. We had fun do with beef and chicken and vegetables. It was very expensive about $100.00 meal for four. Never in my life I ever had or experience anything like it. All this in one day! What a miracle? No? What friends and love and home! These are truly real friends. My family. Community. Everything.

I'M SO HAPPY. I CAN CRY. THIS DAY I WILL NEVER FORGET. SPECIAL. OUR HOUSE.

Dolores: 12th October, 1983.

Catholic Charities O.K. the house. Edwina will sign the contracts Monday. There is so much to be grateful in my new life. It is just the beginning. I have so much to live for.

Dolores: 17th October, 1983.

Edwina signed the house lease today so the house is ours.

Dolores: 21st October, 1983.

The day is just about to end. Everyone is enjoying themselves drinking and eating and laughing. It's a lot of fun. But I guess I really miss drinking, but know I must not take that first drink.

Dear Lord,
Please make - help me get through this feeling. I don't want this drink. I love the way I am now! I don't want to be depressed nor sad. I'm normal. Sometimes I think to myself, why am I an alcoholic? Why me? I must pull myself together. Be happy. Be happy to be sober. Don't be anyone else. Be yourself, "Dolores".

Dolores: 23rd October, 1983.

I finally know how beautiful life is. No way in the world do I want to change my life except being more wiser and mature. I love myself - and God's world that I live in.

Dolores: 26th October, 1983.

I cannot wait to start cleaning the house and fixing it beautiful. This will be my first real home with my own room. All to myself. Everything is going just right for us. Still waiting for a job. But when God thinks it time God will provide a very good job. When the time comes or when it's ready I will get the job.

Dolores.

© 1990. K. Dillow.

PART V: A PLACE TO CALL HOME

26th October, 1983

I have been meaning to write for a long time but somehow life was
going on faster than I could follow up on paper. I should have written
because so much has happened - perhaps all too wondrous to put on
paper at the time!!

We have a house!!!

God's gift became reality in the second week of October. I saw an
advert and called the people who were advertising a house for rent.
We had already seen other places, but this one had something about it,
a something we can call home. I went with Dolores and both of us felt
good about it. It is not as big as we had planned - but it is enough to
begin. There is a basement which has great potential. When God
gives, late though it may seem at the time, God gives in abundance. I
signed the lease on Monday 17th October and today, the 26th, we are
having a house-warming party! The owners left today so we are going
into the house and will start fixing it up. Our party will be held on the
floor, we have no furniture, but....

We have a house!!

We have called it, "Genesis House" to mean 'new beginnings out of
chaos.' **Thank you, God for Genesis House!**

28th October, 1983.

I have a few quiet hours in the forest in Yorkville. It is a warm
afternoon and the last of the leaves are falling. At times like this - a
little time, stolen from the galloping busy hours that fill my week - I
dream again of long stretches of solitude and silence. In this I am most
real and most alive, most aware that this world is God's and that she is
very much present even in all our mess. I know I need a lot of space
and silence. It would be so easy to let everything else take over my

life; nothing else makes sense or gives life if I am not first soaked in the God I find in the forest. It seems to me that everything else follows from that. Dolores is growing in wisdom and maturity every day.

I can hardly believe I fly to London in four days....yes, this time it is hard to go.

CHANGES

Dear God
Be with me,
as I walk your paths,
in places I sometimes
do not want to go.
Be with me
as I say goodbye
to those I want
to stay with.
Be with me
as I leave the gift
so newly given and
hardly seen.
Be with me, Lord
as I try, sometimes sadly,
to walk
your way.

1st November, 1983.

Today I fly to England. I feel no enthusiasm at all - I haven't even packed yet. I am sitting here, unwilling, and even unable to move. It is a wrench now for me to go - everything is happening and I want to be here. Dolores and Ted, who are very enthusiastic, are fixing the house.. Much of the work will have been done by the time I get back, and I feel sad that I won't be able to share these first moments of home creation. I might as well have taken vows of poverty! No, it is not money that poverty refers to, although I have little enough money. I feel the poverty when I have to let go of the creative energy of birthing

Genesis House. I am truly poor when I must allow others to contribute, to create, to form, knowing that all I can do is to try to adjust to it later on. I wouldn't be surprised if Maria and Su put their penny's worth in it as well! How will the "great gift" look when I return?

I said goodbye to good friends. Yes, it is hard to go, but it is time to go. God will use the empty space I leave as well as the place within me which God now cleared. There are many new challenges ahead in these next two months, while I travel through Africa, meeting VMM lay missionaries and all kinds of other people. I pray that God will take care of those I love and especially of my new street friends.

Dolores: 30th November, 1983.

I'm now in Genesis House. I'm officially moved in. I have not written for a month. Well, I have had a few relapses which I feel really bad about. I went all the way down. I guess I was not really as strong as I thought I was. I missed Edwina so much. I could not take it. So I drank. I have not told anyone. But I know they knew. I prayed the other day in Yorkville. I'm straighten up now. I'm starting all over. "AGAIN" going to A.A. Starting from the first step. Why am I so hard-headed?   I hope Edwina will understand, please God, help me to be strong again. Stronger.

Dear Lord,
Please make my life happy. Not lonely. Let me be stronger. I want to so bad.

Dolores: 8th December, 1983.

What can I say or write? Except I did it again and I'm sorry. Why do I do it? I know Edwina will know soon. This is my fourth relapse since she's been gone. I want to be the one to tell her. I cannot put my mind

together now. Because I'm withdrawing now. But I won't hide. I have
to face it. Edwina, I'm so sorry. Please hurry back before I kill myself.
I hate myself.

Dolores.

(Letter written to Dolores by Edwina, dated 18th Dec., 1983)

Dear Dolores,

*I have heard that you have chosen to go back to the streets. Dolores - I
want you to know that I will always love you and that, in spite of where
you are now and what you are doing, I will continue to believe that you
can make it when you choose to do so. I will miss you dearly on the
streets - no one will be able to take your place....but the place will
remain open for you for the day you decide to come home again and
start again with a new program. Every day I pray for you that God
will watch over you and that one day you will start again.*

*I will miss you so much but I do understand that only you yourself can
decide what to do with your life - live it or destroy it. I will never give
up hoping for you, praying for you, loving you....there is nothing more
I can do than this.*

*I feel very sad because I have come to love you dearly and it is very
hard for me to see you dying again. When you decide to start again
we, your friends, will be waiting with great love and with all the
support you need.*

*May God (who never gives up either) take care of you, dear Dolores,
may God help you to find yourself and bring joy to us again.*
    Much love,
        Edwina.

Dolores: 20th December, 1983.

I have come back. It is so good to be welcomed by my friends. They look so beautiful to me!

Dolores: 21st December, 1983.

Dear Lord, Please let me be beautiful again, once more. Please let me show everyone I can make it. And show me. I know I failed numerous times. Please I pray and with everything I got,

From a desperate woman that needs help.

Dolores: 25th December, 1983.

Christmas!

I got so many lovely gifts. What I loved the most was my Koala Bear rug that Edwina got me. I got so many. I, never in my life, have had so many gifts for Christmas.

1. Rug. 2. Perfume. 3. Plaque. 4. Christmas stocking. 5. Key Chain. 6. Calendar. 7. Teddy bear calendars. 8. A miniature Koala bear. 9. Hat and gloves. 10. Picture poster. I was so happy.

Still happy.

Dolores.

9th January, 1984.

Dolores went back to the streets and the drink once again. She is not ready to make a life-giving choice. The decision to stop which she made last year was probably more because of me than Dolores. I read her diary because she wanted me to, and I can see how dependent she has become on me. It is a terrible choice I need to make. Yes, she needs to go through a dependency stage where she can draw strength from me, or anyone else who is strong enough to give. However, Dolores' needs are so great that without my realising it, they had drained me. I became sick with her, and took on her highs and lows, her ups and downs, till I lost my own anchors.

Once again, I am aware that only a community, a team of people, who affirm each other in a caring, healthy and appropriate way, can take on this ministry. However, I cannot put off making the choice of how I am to act with Dolores, because I must act and not continue to react. In a way it is a blessing that I had to go away, and in another it was unfortunate. Dolores needed me, her addiction of choice now, but with me gone she reverted back to her addicition of alcohol. She cannot lie to herself anymore. I cannot continue to enable her to deny her problem. It is unfortunate that she is once more caught in alcohol, but my blessing has been a new objectivity - removing myself from the immediacy of Dolores' problems and struggles has given me greater freedom to face them more calmly, not allowing them to mix in with my own. I too must choose health, otherwise, what could I possibly offer anyone? I must learn more about alcohol and co-dependency to make informed choices. After one year, I feel I am beginning to formulate some questions.

What will 1984 bring? How very different everything seemed this time last year, when I was on the streets alone and quite bewildered, knowing no one nor anything about what it was all about. Now, a year later, we have a house, a small fund, a community of two and a lot of questions that can only be answered in faith and hope. We have a lot to learn, but in the end, it is the women who must teach us. I thank God that so much has been experienced in one short year. I am glad to be going back to the streets. Today we got a tiny wild cat and we called her Genesis.

10th January, 1984.

Dolores came sick and drunk. We talked. She cried. Must we start again? Start again! And again! And again! I feel so broken up inside to see her in the condition she is in. She is dirty, her hair all messed up, and she reeks of alcohol. Yet, I still love her, hope for her, and believe in her. She has blown everything, lost the trust and hope that people put in her. She is a wreck. This is what the ministry is about. Who was it who said our task is to "walk with them from fall to fall until they meet their God"? This is what we must do. It is the quality of the walking-with that is important. Regardless of what I believe, Dolores has a right to be allowed to make choices - even if those choices bring her death. What good would life be if she continues to be dominated and oppressed even by a well-meaning woman like me? Yesterday, Ted and I took Dolores to hospital and they accepted her for DeTox, and possibly another program and then rehabilitation.

I am too tired to write anymore!

14th January, 1984.

Dolores is doing well in the new program. I pray she sticks to it - right through to rehabilitation and halfway house. I am not kidding myself, and know that it will be a major feat to get her to accept that she needs that kind of long-term support. Without it I don't believe she will survive and our little group of two, or the Yorkville community, cannot give her that kind of support. I know Dolores will be a source of great suffering for me as well as for herself. I have come to love her like a daughter, like a sister, and I pray that this love will be life-giving. I must watch that I am not hooked by her addictive manipulation. It can happen so easily.

16th January, 1984.

OMA

Oma was found dead in
her run down hotel room.
She had been dead
three days.
I loved old Oma,

one eyed street lady
from Alabama.
Wrinkled tired face like
a dried up prune.
Thin as a pole,
alcoholic, and
beautiful in her kindness
and gentleness.
Oma -
One blue eye looking out,
terrified,
at an uncaring world.
Oma -
Laughing so readily
through all her pain,
chain smoking,
longing to be a lady
in the slums and the violence of
her inner city world,
peopled with lonely
and bewildered homeless -
like herself.
Oma -
So proud to have found
a room of her own,
at last.
So proud of the dark, cracked walls
because they were hers
to die in.

19th January, 1984.

I spent the day at May's brothel. May sounds full of life and is totally
absorbed in her business which is going well in this cold weather. She
cleared $628.00 on New Year's Eve, after she gave her "ladies" their
share.   There were three women working today.   Irene is out of
hospital, not drunk but not sober. She is living again with Johnny who
has just come out of jail. She is beginning to realise she is being used

by May, by Johnny, who pimps her and by the johns she has to smile at. The love affair with Johnny is over. Irene is trying to be tough about it all. She was so wild and crazy over him a few months ago, and his letters from jail were so passionate and full of promises for their future, but now he is just an alcoholic pimp she cannot bring herself to leave. He is better than being alone. She believes she has no options left.

Lee is a young woman from Tennessee. She is pregnant and is going for an abortion because she does not want a "trick baby". "Never!" she declares vehemently. The baby would be a constant reminder of her oppression. Rene is older than me. She is trying so hard to be seductive and provocative. It is sad when the men constantly ignore her. She has a sixteen-year-old daughter whom she insists must stay at school. "I don't want her to end up like her mother", she tells me.

May gave me $30.00. Fred, one of the tricks who always tries to persuade me to go with him, gave me $10.00 for "my church". I felt God smiling at the incongruency of it all. I feel more comfortable sitting at May's now - it has taken a year!

20th January, 1984.

THE KINGDOM

When you say
Yes
to the Kingdom
things once felt
indispensable
slip by.
One by one
(hardly noticeable at first)
You see them
slip away...
All that you
held on to,

possessed,
claimed,
somehow
disappears,
melts into
another horizon
whilst you are busy
with the new.
You do not notice,
until,
in panic,
you feel
a lonely
searing loss
and look around
afraid.
Yes.
Things have changed.
Suddenly
you want to cry
aloud,
to reclaim,
to re-possess,
to re-establish,
but, oh, you
feel so naked
and different.
The Kingdom,
Ah, yes,
The Kingdom
claims all.

Dolores: 22nd January, 1984

I'm so lonely. More than before, It hurts inside. I'm crying now. I'm
feeling sorry for myself. I don't know what to do.

Dear God, Please take this loneliness from me. Help me to feel better. I don't want to cry nor be lonely. I want joy, hope and happiness. I know it will come later. But I need a little of it now. More than ever. Please listen to my prayers. I know I did wrong in the past and I am making up for it now. Maybe this is a part that I need. But no one knows but you Lord.

Dolores.

23rd January, 1984.

Everything that could happen has happened this week - the car broke down, the gas bill came, the toilet is broken etc. etc. We have no money left. No one seems interested in giving funds for our type of work. They all said, "No". These rejections are a reflection of what society and Church thinks about prostitutes and street women. We are outside all the conventional categories and terms of reference. God had better come up with some bright idea. It was God's idea in the first place! But, for all that, I am glad to be here. And I, the eternal optimist, know we are going to make it. My room is beginning to look lived in. In my absence Maria and Su painted it, put pictures on the wall and curtains on windows and doors. They surprised me, making it a welcome place.

24th January, 1984.

Dolores is doing very well - that gives me great joy. Please Lord, help her make it this time. She could, one day, give so much. We have no money and no prospects for money, but I feel very much at peace. It is all in God's hands - what have we to fear?

Dolores: 25th January, 1984.

Maybe I do need this halfway house. I'm more confused now. I will try to forget it. Just for a while. Now I'm trying to learn more about my alcoholism. That's more important.

It's time for me to grow up and be an adult. I have to take care of Dolores. It's my responsibility and no one else. I cannot have a crutch anymore. I have to pace myself and work out my adult-hood. I'm 28yrs old and I am wanting to be an 8 year old.

Dear God,
Please help me make the right decision. I want to do what is best. I don't want to be hurt. I'm tired of being a rubber ball. Thank you for this day and my sobriety. Love you. Also my community.
        Dolores.

2nd February, 1984.

Dolores is going to the halfway house. We are grateful to the God who is watching so closely over her. Ted and I took her to visit the place. It is small, a little shabby, but friendly and comfortable. Just what Dolores needs! She is going to make it!

There will be a rose growing on the Broadway...

Ted and I spent last night, sleepless, in the shelter. Oh, the despair and the sadness. Cochise was there, with all the noble look of his Indian tribe, utterly down and degraded, a broken man who a few generations ago would have been a splendid hunter and warrior. Marie, "his squaw", as she calls herself, inseparable from Cochise, staggering around in baggy jeans, desperate and stinking. She should have been a beautiful and proud Indian woman, standing beside her man. What have we done? Most of us still believe the Hollywood myth that the Indians were the "baddies" who attacked the peaceful settlers. We don't know how we invaded the land, desecrated all that was holy and pretended it all belonged to us - ready for the taking. We are adamant about defending our land - but we say the Indians were wrong in defending theirs. Now that we took all that was meaningful we relegate them to the ranks of the invisible people in reservations or in the streets. Oh, there is so much terrible sadness on these streets. Dolores - make it! I am very tired. I need a little quiet time for God and for myself.

Dolores: 2nd February, 1984.

It's now midnight. I feel very happy and good inside. I did it. The halfway house was for me. I made a decision. I want to go.

Dolores: 5th February, 1984

Lord I need it so bad. I need to learn more. I have a lot still to grow and with this program I have faith that I will make it.

Dolores: 6th February, 1984.

Feeling great now. It happened. I got accepted in the halfway house. I'm so, so happy. So relieved. I cannot wait till I go. I can feel that I'm going to grow so much from this halfway house.

Dolores: 8th February, 1984.

I must learn to live my own life again. No one can live it for me, but Dolores.

I can see three pictures in my head -

1. I can see Yorkville lovely fresh, clean, my community.
   Quietness.

2. I can see Chicago. In my room with my community.
   Also my home, my life, my family.

3. I can see darkness with red deep red flashes and arms.
   Dozens of arms reach out to me, and I saw them as
   my enemy.

8th February, 1984.

Once again I sit in the brothel. Would God sit here too? Would the so called "good" people sit here with me? Will we sit here doing nothing but bringing ourselves and hopefully our love to places where people are? We have preached and moralized enough. Now it is time to sit with the pain, to sit with those who are hurting too deeply to listen or care about our preaching.

Catherine is back. She looks thinner and sadder. She had gone to her mother's and had left Peter, but she tells me she has now returned to him. Why? It still amazes me how women who were abused in any way as children, spend their lives seeking and preserving, once found, relationships that only repeat the pattern of abuse they have always known. They are afraid - afraid to be alone, or afraid to be beaten or hurt or sent to jail. They are afraid of allowing themselves to be just themselves, because they are afraid that they are really monsters inside.

Rene came in ill-kempt and tense. May swore at her. May has so much bitterness and anger in her and she uses the women to vent it out. The first guy refused Rene, and Catherine had to go instead. Rene was all broken up about it. She was fighting not to cry and was looking so, so unhappy. I felt quite helpless, what a joyless place. This might just be a glimpse of hell, sad, negative, unhappy and angry people staying with each other, because they do not know there are other places to go to and other people to meet. May curses on, surrounded by broken people. Hell!

9th February, 1984.

I picked Dolores up from the hospital and brought her back to Yorkville. This is her new beginning. I think she will make it. She is growing. It is so good, so encouraging to see her sober and happy. It is worth it all! It is a sign of hope for others and for us.

13th February, 1984.

Dolores has been with us these past few days and tomorrow we are taking her to the halfway house. She is happy, sober and enthusiastic. Oh, she will grow so much if she is able to stick to it. I feel so good about Dolores - what a long haul it has been, but how worthwhile it is to see the new woman she is becoming! Mark (Gypsy) is still with us at Yorkville. He is such a beautiful person too, and a joy to be with, when he is sober.

Dolores:13th February, 1984.

Tomorrow is the day! I'm very anxious about going. A little scared. 3 months. First time I been away for this long since I left boarding school. I am happy. I'm sober and I do have a lot going for me. I'm no better than anyone. I'm just myself sober and beautiful. It all takes one day at a time.
Lord, Thank you for these 24hrs and for this new beginning. I love. I pray for the alcoholics and co-alcoholics.

The end and a new beginning and a new life.

Dolores.

22nd February, 1984

Busy! Busy! Busy! Loving God, please keep me attentive to your silence and presence. Dolores is still a source of concern. She is having a tough time and is really on a down. It seems there is nothing left we can do except pray that she won't give up. If she leaves the program, I know she will not make it. She isn't ready to face a sober life yet. Dear God, sustain her. She has come so far.

I went to May's in the afternoon for a couple of hours. Rene was sad and depressed. She's not getting the dates. All the guys go for Catherine or Vicky. She must feel so neglected but she pretends to be absorbed in her thriller novel. May is ruthless and scornful.

Catherine's face is all swollen and bruised - Peter beat her up. Why do these women go through all this? To really help, we need to prevent our children being abused and hurt. Surely they are the responsibility of all of us, not just their parents. When will we wake up? We pretend we don't do anything because we want to respect people's private lives - but who protects the children?

Dolores: 20th February, 1984.

I'm confused. I'm getting that strange feeling within myself. That running feeling. I been acting very childish. Sometimes I feel like saying the Hell with everything and everybody. But I cannot. Because I love my family. So you see I cannot give up.

Dolores: 22nd February, 1984.

Dear Lord,
Thank you so much for these 24 hours. I pray for Edwina and VMM. Also Lord I would like to pray for myself that I grow and find this place as my home and my family. And please forgive me for acting like this and hurting the people I love. Lord I don't want to lose any of them.

Thank you Lord.

Please hear me. Dolores.

23rd February, 1984.

I talked with Mark (Gypsy) today and he told me something I won't forget easily. "I hate people - people hurt - I like the cat better than people. Cats don't hurt you, like people do. It's the good ones - the ones you think are okay - that hurt the most."

Mark has been so hurt that he has built up a great wall around him so he won't be vulnerable or hurt anymore. We challenge, and disturb him because we turn upside down all his experiences with people who have been negative and hurtful. We confuse him with our love. He questioned what he is doing in return for his keep here at the house where he is staying with us. I told him his presence and friendship are enough. He doesn't know what to do with that. I told him, "Mark, quit running away from yourself." He admits he is afraid. He is afraid to love - but his confusion is good. At least he is now at the stage where he is struggling with it.

Our conversation reminded me of one I had with one of the prostitutes, Vicky, yesterday. She was vehement - "I hate all people - give me animals anyday...." She was consumed with anger and pain. The common thread is HURT. Only God's grace can break through such pain. I wish we could begin to understand how these women have been abused and hurt and how they contribute to the continuation of their own abuse in their lives. I wish we were a compassionate people, like our compassionate Mother God.

27th February, 1984. Gloucester, Mass.

OCEAN

By the ocean,
enormous rocks
studded with shining pebbles.
The water seeps
and sucks in
smooth harmony.
I can hear
the gulls
screaming in the
empty sky,
and a tug
churns its way
back to the harbor.
There is God
in the rocks,
the water,

the gulls and
the tug....
There is God
shining,
sweeping,
streaming....
God
chugging
thru' this world
un-noticed,
un-remarked.
God soaked Godself
in the world
when God fashioned it.

Dolores: 1st March, 1984.

I can feel myself growing and maturing. I have a lot to think while I'm
here. I'm starting to find myself and my needs and what I want in the
future.

The days are going fast
Soon it will be Spring time.
The flowers and
birds will be out.
But I have to keep in mind
one day at a time.

Dolores: 2nd March, 1984.

What I do need is to get in touch with God I have so much to be
thankful for.

Dolores: 5th March, 1984.

As I think back how much I hurt Edwina and the people I love so much. How stupid I was.

"My dear Lord, Thank you for this 24 hours that was a sober one. Thank you for everything today. For the food and bed and shelter. I like to pray for the ladies here. Also like to pray for the sick and needy in other countries."

Dolores: 8th March, 1984.

Am I going backwards? Why do I do things wrong? I know I'm not mature yet. Not fully. I want to be grown. Maybe I try too hard. I don't want to hurt anybody anymore. I just want to be Dolores.

I see Dolores as a good person, not mean at all, and not a snob. I want to be somebody.

Dear Dolores,
I'm writing this letter to let you - give yourself a chance, to know yourself better. You're not looking on the brighter side of your life. You got a whole new life in front of you, don't throw it away. You are somewhere, growing, Dolores. Not saying you will never be a part of them. But now Dolores, don't cry. Because I know you. Just look at the good in you. Also Dolores, I know you feel hurt, rejected and lonely. But you're not. You are loved by many people, especially by God. I know you will miss Edwina. But just remember she loves you and love always grows however far that person is. It even grows more. Dolores, you are a very fortunate woman.

So pray my Dolores.
O.K. Love you.
        Love,
            God.

Dear God,

I do understand that I do have a wonderful life ahead of me. Yes you are right. I will miss Edwina but I will not get depressed. Maybe a little lonely. But I will know she will be back and you are right. Love does grow stronger, when a person is gone a while.

Thank you God for your letter. You opened my eyes and heart to see and feel how others feel. I must remember I am not the only one that has feeling.

> Love,
> Dolores.

SOBRIETY
(by Dolores)

I love being sober.
Sober for me is like being
born all over again.
Like a seed that grows into
a beautiful Rose.

Sobriety.
Sober is smelling good
all over.
A beautiful fragrance that has
a scent of a garden after it
rains and the sunshine is out.

Sobriety -
is cleanness and neatness.

Sobriety -
is when you have real
friends that you care
for and care for you.

Dolores: 16th March, 1984.

I pray for all the miracles I have because I believe I am a Miracle.

Dolores: 18th March, 1984.

Lord, I want to be good and sober. I'm scared Lord because I have lost something that was a part of me and I'm trying to put another piece in that lost part that is missing. Because living on the streets and drinking did play the major part in my life. Please help me find that piece. There is only one part that can fit that part, and I know it is sobriety and caring friends.

Dolores: 22nd March, 1984.

My morning was good except now I feel a little down for some odd reason. I'm sitting in my room looking at my corner of my room where I can say it is my corner. Today I made my little corner my room (Home) and I love it. I have a lot of pretty things I got to be thankful for. I have things I never had before in my life from friends, good friends, real ones, not fake nor false friendship. The ladies here were telling me I have a lot of things for a person that lived on the streets, and I do. Just thinking how one year has pass, and all the friends and gifts I have gotten actually. If I had not met Edwina I would not have met VMM. A little over than a year ago I did not have any real friends. I'm so happy I can cry.

I have my God which I call my Higher Power, and it is about time we had a talk (a serious talk). When I go to Yorkville we walk together in the beautiful nature there.

Anyways, I like walking. I need the time away by myself.

Alone.... Alone is good.

You don't have to be sad, nor depressed to be alone.

Alone is being with me. Sharing to myself. I don't think it is selfish. I think it is a part of me that belongs to no one but me (Dolores).

Dolores: 25th March, 1984.

How long will my sobriety last? I don't want to give it up.

Lord, thank you for 24hrs forgiving me for thinking this. I know you understand what I'm going through. It is a very hard struggle for me. I thank you for helping me this far.

Dolores: 26th March, 1984.

I'm feeling sorry for myself. I want out. It's beautiful. I want to go to Chicago. But I cannot make that decision because I know what I'm liable to do and I do not want to go backwards. But what can I do? I prayed this morning. Maybe a little harder.

Dear God,
Help me through this day.

Dolores: 28th March, 1984.

As I think back, a year ago I was going through a lot of changes with Edwina. It was a lot of fears, hurts and pains because I never had anybody who cared for me.

Dolores: 9th April, 1984.

How I wish I can get rid of these pains I have. They are in my gut about how I feel about leaving. I'm still confused.

Lord, please help me through my struggles. Thank you for helping me through these 24hrs. I need strength to help me through my burdens. I have not been so honest with my sisters. Please forgive me.

Thank you, Lord. Love,
        Dolores.

11th April, 1984. Chicago.

It's now 3.00 a.m. in the night shelter. We filled up quickly tonight,
like other nights. All is quiet except for a variety of loud snores. It is
so sad to see so many homeless people sleeping in these awful
conditions on the church floor....sad, sad, sad.

Mark has gone back to the streets. He is very abusive and agressive.
He is on the defensive and, of course, drunk. Everyone he has loved in
life has left him. He blames himself for his wife's death. If he hadn't
been drinking the paramedics would have realized that she wasn't
drunk and that she was bleeding inside. Instead they smelled the
alcohol and left her to die which she did, 24 hrs later. And Mark
couldn't scream, couldn't claim his and her right to be taken to hospital
and treated. For him the world will always be alien and hostile, and he
drinks to make sure he remains invisible and invulnerable. But, how
he loved her! How much he misses her still!!

People like Dolores and Mark, are caught in a vicious cycle. Dolores
needs a job, but to get and keep a job, she needs motivation and
discipline. At this moment Dolores' motivation for a job is non-
existent. She doesn't have the middle-class mentality that describes
people by what they do. She does not perceive a job as describing her,
or giving her dignity, or any of the other subtle perks. She does not see
it as giving herself power over her life. A job for her means money,
money she doesn't feel she needs. At best her motivation is pleasing
me. Even if we were to "educate" her in the life-giving meaning of
labor, all she is trained for is a meaningless job. Even is she did get a
job, Dolores has spent her life seeking instant gratification, and when
that was not possible, she drank to obliterate the need. She has not
been secure enough in her life and relationships to wait in peace for
something she wants. A meaningless job does not provide much
gratification - and certainly what it does provide is not instant. How
can we make up for the lack of security so she can learn to delay her
need to be gratified?

"God have compassion on your people. They are so lost and so lonely and frightened". I read in the shelter log book that Marie (Cochise's wife) has died, probably from a combination of alcohol and Dilantan. She was such a gentle soul. She and Cochise were inseperable. Maybe she wanted to die. I believe a lot of these people do.

I am tired now. It is time to wake the next shift.

12th April, 1984.

JOE WHITE EAGLE

Joe White Eagle
staggered into the basement shelter
drunk and stinking.
A red woollen hat
was pulled over
his half-closed blackened eye,
and his dirty sweater was
frayed and too short.
He wore baggy trousers
that shone
with years of grease.
Staggering,
grinning,
eyes unfocused,
Joe White Eagle
marked a cross
on the sign-on sheet,
and dragged
his thin foam mattress
towards the center of
the basement floor.
The coffee in the
fragile styrofoam cup
spilled onto the cement floor,
as Joe

bent clumsily forward
to pull off his heavy
lace-less boots.
"Ah - what the hell",
He gave up and
collapsed, exhausted,
fully clothed, on
the mattress and
the styrofoam cup.
All around him
the foul smell of
unwashed bodies and
dirty clothes
arose, and filled
the basement shelter.
Coughing, spluttering,
spitting, snoring....
The homeless and
the derelicts
fell into
troubled, lonely sleep.
Joe White Eagle,
derelict,
bum,
drunk,
sprawled in pitiful heap
on the shelter's
cold grey floor,
senseless,
pathetic figure
of utter despair , and
degradation.
Morning came.
It was a sharp,
cold day.
Only the gulls
and a lone jogger
broke the still air
with movement.

The lake was hushed
and flat,
filled with millions
of sparkling suns.
The breeze
barely whispered
over the vast
shining waters.
Etched darkly
against the silver lake,
great and bottomless,
in a lotus position,
a lonely figure sat,
lost
inside himself,
absorbed in
another world,
another life,
swept up in
the deep of the lake and
the vastness of the sky.
A sudden breeze
playfully brushed
his dark shining hair
and there,
bronzed and noble,
face lifted up
to the pale, pale sun,
Joe White Eagle
sat
proud and un-surrendered,
son and brother,
of his native land and lake.
Joe White Eagle,
hunter and warrior
on the great empty plains,
lost in a thousand dreams
of dignity and
dying splendor.

Joe White Eagle sat
proud and un-surrendered.

Dolores: 13th April, 1984.

I'm trying to feel more happier of myself. Maybe it is time for me to
go (Run). No! I have to learn to stop running away from my problems
every time I get upset about something. I just have to deal with the
problem and that is exactly what I will do. But why do I get that
emotionally upset so easily? Am I that fragile?

18th April, 1984. Chicago.

Irene is in hospital again. I visited her and Johnny in their hotel room a
few days ago and Irene was sick in bed and in great pain. I drove her
to the medical center and from there she was transferred to hospital. I
have visited her each day. She is well cared for, but her liver is in bad
condition. It is not surprising for someone who drinks over a gallon of
sherry wine every day. Visiting Irene in the hospital gives me the
opportunity to talk with her in depth. We talked about her life. She
got into drugs - heroin - at sixteen and then to prostitution to support
her habit. "I couldn't do it unless I was high or drunk." I really believe
what she says because I have heard so many women say the same
thing. She told me of some of the things the men ask for and I believe
most women would have to be high to go through that!

After visiting Irene, I went to the brothel. "Nicky", alias Marie, shared
a bit with me. She used to be a "counsellor" with difficult girls at the
boarding school Dolores went to. Her real job was as home help but
with her own history of sexual abuse as a child, she identified with
many of the residents. It is not suprising that she is now a hooker, is
behind in her rent, and having a difficult time of it.

Lorraine was there too. She is the first 'housewife hooker' I have met.
"Something to fall back on", she says, "to make ends meet." Her
husband is sick and unemployed, and they have three children. She
says she has tried to get other work with no luck. "I wouldn't do this

unless I had to." She has applied for a job at Woolworths and is hoping to get it. Economic poverty and female oppression have a lot to do with women getting into prostitution. I have not yet met the mythical "happy hooker". Business seems bad for the women lately. Nobody seems to know why. Police are picking them up more regularly so they have to keep moving about. The johns seem to have been scared too. Maria sat in court for Genesis House, the other day and 20 johns were there and about 10 of the women. Not one of the men got a fine, but the women did. There was one man who asked the judge to have his bail money sent to a lawyer rather than his house so his wife wouldn't find out about it. The judge agreed! Society has a sick set of values when we come to prostitution.

19th April, 1984.

Yesterday I visited May's and I experienced the old familiar sense of despair and hopelessness as I sat in the lounge. There were five women working, all run-down and seedy. Two were exceedingly overweight and most unattractive, but they were trying so hard to look coquettish, with heavy make-up and inappropriate skimpy clothes. I felt very, very sad for them - May told me that a senior Police Officer was one of the day's clients. What the hell! On one hand the police harass them and on the other they use them. What games we play!

The men that came in were mostly middle-aged, overweight and pathetic. What a dismal destructive place! I talked to some of the tricks. There was Vince, who wants to take me out to lunch and seems very curious about me. He asks a lot of questions about God, confession, conversion etc. Interesting! I don't want to go out with him at all, but feel I should be open. What is his game, I wonder? there was also Mario, an Italian, quiet and relaxed. Al, looked like a university professor, definitely a professional. May and the girls call him "Kissbug", because he goes in for a lot of kissing. I still find it hard to be comfortable with the men. I am another nameless, invisible object to them, with whom they cannot play the same sex games.

I had some good conversations with the women about pimps and why and how they get caught up with them. Lee had one for three years and is now very tough and bitter about it all. She knows she was abused. These girls get harder and tougher with every rejection. Catherine is once again leaving Peter and trying to set herself up in her own apartment. She has spent all her money on his drugs for the last few years. She is beginning to realise how much better she could do for herself if she took care of herself and saved. But will she stick to it? There is a whole universe between the women becoming aware of their oppression and their ability to do something to change it. It takes years to make the right choices that eventually lead to healing and wholeness.

Today, I came to the forest to get back some perspective. In the streets, the bars, and brothel, it is easy to lose the balance and the harmony.

GOOD FRIDAY

I went into the forest,
and in all the death
of these past months,
I saw
new life,
thrusting forward,
everywhere.
Everywhere I looked,
the whole earth
was heaving,
giving birth,
among the dead leaves
and in broken earth!
The stream
sprang fresh, clear water,
gurgling
like a baby
in new discovered joy.
And the birds
were quite silly

in their unrestrained
screeches, and
long pitched notes.
Everything,
everywhere,
was calling aloud,
LIFE!
And in all the
thrusting and
singing and
laughter,
I heard
a flower
grow.

Sitting by the water in the forest is a confessional experience. I steep myself in the harmony and truth of God's creation and realise how unharmonious and dishonest I can be. It is important and necessary, therefore, to be still and silent in the womb of the forest. As I become one with its truth I become deeply aware of what I am called to become.

CALLED TO BE

I am called to be beautiful.
As clear as this stream,
I am reborn as deep,
as nourishing as this earth,
I am taught to be as wise,
as strong as these trees,
I am loved into becoming
as harmonious,
as honest as all this creation.
It is important,
necessary therefore,
to watch the worm,

as it busies itself in the earth
where it belongs.
God, Creator/Creation,
Accomodates
and receives us
like that.
We are called
to be enveloped
and consumed into
the Godhead,
but we are afraid
to bury
very deep.
We could learn a lot
just from the worm.
The worm is blind,
but she knows where her life is..

Dolores: 20th April, 1984.

Feeling better. I was myself today kinda down. But it is O.K.
Looking forward to tomorrow, which I feel is frightening. Not the fact
that I might drink because I do not know what I might do. Because I
am a Alcoholic and I know how I am. I just have to be careful Oh
when I think of my last drunk. Them dirty streets. Myself dirty. Even
the insanity part, fears me. I know I can make it.

"Lord, Thank you for this day even though I'm hurting I will do my
best to be the person you want me to be. I need you on my side."

Dolores: 22nd April, 1984.

"Dear Lord, Thank you for today's struggles. Looking forward to
celebrating your Resurrection in the morning. Lord help me."

Easter Sunday night:
I am grateful for these 24 hours sobriety. Is this what I am supposed to
be grateful for? I don't want to be here Lord. It is a hard struggle. I
need your help before I go to pieces. I will do anything. I cannot stop
thinking about leaving. I have to talk to my counselor in the morning.
I am going to tell her. I am ready to make plans. My plan is drink,
relapse, plan and counter relapse! I cannot help thinking of every
angle to take. Easy way out. Am I planning my drunk, or am I in my
stress period? I HAVE TO TALK WITH SOMEONE.

Dolores: 23rd April, 1984.

Dearest Lord,
I pray for the strength and hope throughout this day because I am
starting some naughty thinking. I feel I want to leave now. Today -
half of me say go for it. The other half says fight it Dolores, you can
do it. Lord help me. Should I go out? I will go out because this will
be one of many times that I will get these feelings. Just tell me, give
me a sign that I know I will get through this terrible stress that I am
going through.

Night.....
My feelings are better. My health is better. I went to get a liver profile
and blood drawn. I'm feeling 50% better. "Hey, I made it!" I am so
happy this day is over with.

> Love,
> Dolores.

25th April, 1984. Chicago.

I'm back at May's. I don't know how much more of this negativity I
can take. It is so easy to say that I will work with the women where
they are, but how long can I remain in this hell without becoming part
of it? There is so much verbal abuse, tearing one another to pieces.
Never a kind word, kindness is alien, foreign! Back-biting is rampant,
but all of this covered over with a veneer of humor, sometimes very

funny, sometimes cruel. This is a far cry from the silence and peace of the forest.

But God, I believe, is equally present here. Here God hurts and cries. In the forest God sings and laughs, but in both places God loves.

Dolores: 25th April, 1984.

I'm alone. Nobody is here except me. All the ladies are out on this gorgeous day. The staff are at a workshop so here I am sitting behind the desk taking phone messages. It is so peaceful here. The quietness! It is good to be alone. I needed this peace and tranquility of the mind. I am doing a lot of planning and thinking. No naughty thinking! The morning was beautiful. Looking forward to a good evening at the seminar. No tears this morning. Just happy smiles.

Dolores.

26th April, 1984.

Rene is back at the brothel. She is dressed in a skimpy, violently-colored cotton dress, her hair bleached a harsh yellow, track marks and bruises all down her arms. She looks so sad! Sometimes all these girls make is $10.00 - $20.00 per day. Other times it may be $100.00 - but who knows? They live on a knife edge of fear and insecurity. Catherine is as cool and beautiful as ever. "She'll do anything", say the other girls, "she's the only one who will do anything the guys want." "I don't know why she does it", protests Lee. Lee has her boundaries very clearly marked - no man will do certain things with her! "Those kind of women who will do anything", says Lee, "are the ones who can only survive with alcohol or drugs." It is an emotionally brutal and brutalising place. The girls talk freely with me, but I have to accept that I do not know whether my presence makes any difference or not. Last week, May told one of the tricks, "I feel a completely different woman when she (me) is here." I wonder if that is really true. If it is, what is she borrowing from me? Am I used by her to ease the pain of guilt? Do I act as an official representative of church and society, giving absolution to a destructive lifestyle? Or am I one of the few people who has loved her and seen beyond what she does to who she is?   Prostitution is a hard and violent life.   Except, perhaps occasionally, for a high-class call-girl. For most it is a life of utter desperation and self-destruction. The humaness, the warmth, the gentleness, the tenderness, the caring that makes us women is diminished, destroyed or distorted.

Prostitution, in whatever form it takes, means the selling of the best of ourselves to another for some temporary gain. It can be our bodies, our brain, our hands, One "merchandise" is not really different from the other. It is not really what we do, but what motivates us to do it. What prostitution really does is to compromise the values which give meaning to our lives. When we do so, our lives become empty and senseless. We then live in shame and in guilt. If society affirms these concepts of ourselves, we find our low image of ourselves justified. In our Western society, selling our brains and our hands is actually commended. We sell ourselves to industry, to government and get rewards....but the human cost is the same.

5th May, 1984.

Dolores relapsed today. She was taken to DeTox.

6th May, 1984.

Dolores has gone back to the streets. I am in the forest, bruised, hurting, anxious. I have brought my pain to the trees, to the new young plants, to the fresh buds, and they all shout to me - LIFE!

Life, right in the middle of my dying. I grieve amongst these symbols of life. I must carry the pain until the God of the forest bursts through it, and transforms it into great, great grace. Not yet. I have to caress the hurt until it becomes me.

DOLORES

Dolores,
dear one,
with your chewed-up,
over-kissed
teddy bear
stuffed in your pocket.
Dolores,
dear one,
with your new young dreams,
trailing in bits
behind you.
Dolores,
dear one,
lumbering up the Broadway,
drowning your
knots of despair,
in deep,
red wine.
Dolores,
dear one -
don't die.

I cannot do anything more - only prayer and fasting.

HEALING

The pain and the wounds
go too deep
for us to heal
alone.
Only God,
only a
far Greater Power
can penetrate
such depth

> of pain,
> and gently, gently,
> sooth,
> and kiss us
> to wholeness.
> It is too much
> for us,
> all of it has to be
> given over
> entirely
> to God.
> All of it.

7th May, 1984.

Dolores came back tonight - not sober, but weepy and repentant. She is sleeping here tonight, but tomorrow we must talk seriously with her and clarify the boundaries. We call it "tough love". Finally I am in a place where I am no longer willing to enable the drinking. Her choosing to drink has consequences she needs to face up to. It is the only way in which we can show we respect her enough to respect her choice, even if we cannot help her go through with it.

8th May, 1984.

Dolores walked out this morning and is back on the streets, drinking. How far must we see her go down before she decides to live? It is so hard to watch. We can only pray.

9th May, 1984.

Today was Dolores' birthday. She had talked about it so much. We had bought her a bicycle.....ah, well. Ted and I went to see Dolores' counsellor. She was a great help and encouragement to us, reinforcing the "tough love". We have to remove all the props and supports from Dolores, even our telephone conversations, so that, ultimately, she will be alone. Then, it will be herself and God. She must face herself and her God, and we must take ourselves out of the way for that to happen.

Oh, it is so hard! I have come to love and treasure Dolores so much. I must stand and watch her die while I pray for her living.

"Mother God - hold her closely and set alight within her the tiny spark of grace which will tell her she can make it. I did not know I could be so vulnerable."

10th May, 1984.

A quiet day, more through preoccupation than design. There is a knot in my heart for Dolores. I pray not only that will God hold her and heal her, but that God will also hold and heal me.

MOTHER GOD

Mother God,
let your great compassion
burst upon Dolores,
whom I love.
Hold her, heal her.
Don't allow her
to give up.
Whisper hope and
love to her.
Let your whisper
dissolve
and banish
the utter darkness
in which she cries.
Oh, Mother,
save this precious child.
The days are heavy.
Be compassionate, mighty God.

Yes, have pity on us
in this darkness,
pain and
sadness.
Oh - the rip inside of me!
Driving past Pigeon Square,
late at night,
there she was,
all alone,
hunched up on a bench,
in the darkness,
with traffic speeding past
her misery.
I nearly choked
with the pain I felt,
as I looked at her.
O God,
let it be tonight,
let your healing,
loving power,
seize her.
Let her whisper - "Yes!"
Let her shout - "Yes!"
Let her cry aloud - "Oh, Yes!
I will live!"
Sit with her
in Pigeon Square.
Mother God.

13th May, 1984

I was invited to give homilies at a parish in the suburbs and told the women in the brothel. "Girls", declared May, "Edwina's preaching - we're going!" I was stunned, horrified at the thought of a pew full of prostitutes and their madam sitting in the middle of the church listening to me preach. "Oh no, oh no - don't travel all that way....", I protested, and then dropped the subject.

The following Sunday, I climbed up the steps to the altar. As I made the sign of the cross before the people, I saw them, May and the row of prostitutes, waving and grinning in a middle pew. I heard God laughing! During Communion I saw the people climb over the women sitting in the pew, as they hastened into the aisle to go up to the front. May and the women remained transfixed in their places. After Eucharist was over, I went up to my friends huddling in the vestibule. "Why didn't you go to Communion?", I asked. May leant over conspirationally and whispered, "Edwina, we didn't confess." "Neither", I felt in my heart, "did we." "Well", said May in satisfaction, "we missed a morning's business, but it was worth it."
And God smiled.

14th May, 1984.

I took Ann to hospital to see her "old man", Vince, who nearly died with an overdose of drugs. Ann is a big Indian woman, and it was very moving to see how gentle she became when she was with Vince. She loves him, in spite of all the drugs, the violence, the poverty. Only a few weeks ago, Vince beat Ann up very badly. Now she holds and caresses him and speaks with great tenderness. She tells me that she knows of his pain; the violence and abuse he suffered as a child. She doesn't pretend she can take it away, but she is willing to forgive him over and over again. She recognizes in him her own pain, and so identifies with him that his violence becomes her own. She thinks so little of herself that it is not hard to think of him as great. In Ann and Vince I see the marriage of a common pain, the pain of being invisible in our world.

I saw Dolores, crashed in the Women's Drop-In Center. She shunned this place and saw it as fit only for women who are at the bottom of the pile. Now she is in the very same place she said she could never go back to. What will she feel in her heart when she wakes up and, in a moment of clarity, realises where she is and what she is doing?

16th May, 1984.

May's venom was spilling out today. She kept repeating, "Kill them!" "Kill them all!" "Them", being a whole anonymous group of people, whores, addicts, welfare exploiters, drug pushers, all the people she hates. Her heart is so hardened! Catherine is nervous and tense because she has given May a false address. She does not want May to know where she is living. Catherine called me tonight for the first time in the eighteen months I have known her and we talked for half an hour. It has taken a long time. But now there is a little sign of hope and communication. Rene is now staying with Lloyd because he is so dependent on her. Rene is a junkie, looking old and very frightened, but she wants to convince herself that he needs her and wants her. Catherine was chosen by the three men who came in this morning. Rene had no business until this afternoon when Catherine suggested to her client that he invite Rene too and have a threesome. Irony. The compassionate prostitute reaching out to the rejected one. Rene is on her way out, but to what? Death as a junkie? What else is there for a spent, penniless prostitute? "God can you break through that?"

Tonight, Dolores called. This was her first call after we set boundaries. She was asking for help to get to DeTox. I said no, she could get there herself. I told her we loved her, but that she must do it herself. There was a second call, from DeTox this time. She made it! I told her we would see her in 48 hours, Friday. I leave her in God's hands. "Take care of her, O Mother God, let her make it! Hold her fast. Thank you for a day's blessings."

I am learning very slowly.

20th May, 1984.

Today is my birthday!! I sit by the stream in the forest. Everything is riotous in its new young growth. The birds are going crazy in their song. I can smell the grass and the new young leaves. I think of Dolores, the squalor, the misery. I have to smell the lilac. I ask the God of the lilac, the God of the birds, and the God of the fresh new leaves, to go to the dirty sidewalk, where Dolores slumps. Let her there smell the lilacs - Ah - smell the lilacs, Dolores!

ECCENTRIC LOVE

Mother God!
How magnificent is your creation.
I see the birds,
flashes of red and blue
darting through the forest,
spilling glorious song
into the air.

I see the print of the beaver
in the drying mud
at the edge of the stream,
and see the new burst butterflies
dancing over the shining water.
And all this wondrous life
sings your praises!
I sit amongst it
attentive to the kiss
of the breeze and the thrusting spring
bursting around me.

I sit in awe
that I am part,
a central part
of such an outspread
of excessive,
eccentric love.

Tonight I went up to the shelter for an hour - and as always found it sad and dis-spiriting.

22nd May, 1984.

THE OFFERING

On my altar before God
there is a small plate with
three squares of cheese and
a slice of summer sausage,
half a glass of gin and tonic,
and a red candle burning.
They are like offerings, pathetic, human,
but very much me
and all I have at this time....

I think - how does God feel
about my cheese and sausage and gin?
Will God see them made holy,
because I think of Her
as I gaze on them,
rather sadly, wistfully -
perhaps longing for incense, starched cloth,
and the musky air
or a darkened church corner?

Will God receive my longing
and my dreams
through these lonely leftovers
which spiralled my little soul
to thoughts of love and redemption?

Cheese, summer sausage,
gin and a red candle
burning, reflecting,
the fleeting glance
of an all touching God.

23rd May, 1984.

I went to May's. Only Lee and Catherine were there and they had no customers while I was visiting. Catherine was very quiet. Lee was playing it tough and was clearly bored. Then I visited Irene in her hotel room. Johnny was sprawled out on the bed drunk. Irene and I went out to eat. Irene insisted on paying as she had made $25.00 "in two minutes" today.

Afterwards I brought her over to Genesis House and we sat and chatted for a couple of hours. It was good, but Irene will not stop drinking. It is sad to see another young and beautiful woman dying. She hinted at her well-to-do family with their big houses, important jobs and impressive cars. She goes to see them sometimes, but they have no idea of her lifestyle. How would a wealthy upper middle-class family handle a daughter who had become a street prostitute?

> I have seen
> no joy
> today
> and seen
> no hope
> today,
> but experienced
> a little faith.

29th May, 1984.

Dolores is still drinking on the streets. She will never know perhaps, how much she is missed and loved and how much I long for life for her. Gypsy Mark is in Yorkville and sober. I rejoice in this ministry, this calling, but often it hurts. In a few days I will be going to the trailer on retreat - I look forward to that very much. I need to be alone with the God who nourishes and calls.

"Bring Dolores to life, dear God - please. Ah, there is so much death around here.

Desperate moments...
trust...
believe... believe...
become the mustard seed!"

30th May, 1984.

Rene was there when I got to May's today. She was dressed in clothes
too tight, too short and too young for her. May told me she comes
from a farming family in Minnesota and left home at seventeen. She
does not like to talk about herself, but gives forth a continuous and
bitter narrative about everyone and everything in her life. No one
escapes her violent tongue. I wonder what she says about me? Still,
she receives me graciously.

GOD IN THE BROTHEL

I went to the brothel
and took God
with me.
The Madam cursed and spat
fury and hatred,
spewing it out
all over the kitchen
and all over God.
The girls sat listless,
in dreadful despair,
waiting for the customers,
with their dirty minds,
and cold, cold lust.
The men,
furtive and awkward,
in their smart business suits,
itching to rape,
and to steal,
before driving home

to the wife and kids,
and barbecue
on the lawn.
I went to the brothel
and found God
within.
And, through all
the sickness,
the sin, and
the stink,
God sat,
in stunned and dreadful
silence.

2nd June, 1984.

I am in the hermitage at Yorkville. It is a long time since I have stayed
in the hermitage. It brings back so many memories of the long months
spent here.....and all that that led me to....who would have thought!!

GOD'S BOSOM

Though nothing appears to happen and
no God speaks,
we have to believe
in the powerful action, wrought
in silence and darkness,
through God's grace.
Faith
sees nothing,
yet believes
everything.
It is good to be in
the silence which is,
deep, deep, deep,
and feel the

strength and the warmth
of the Earth,
my Mother.
I am embraced
by the silence and
the Earth.
Everything here
is true.
I need to breathe
the Truth
deeply,
because our world is filled
with so many lies,
and so much deceit.
We, perhaps,
without even noticing,
let Truth
slip away from us.
But the Earth,
and the tiny violet,
will remind us,
and softly stir
the God within us
to joyful recognition
and harmony.

I delight
in the Earth,
and kiss
the violet.
So, then,
does God.
So close,
so close is God,
that when
we stoop
to stroke the Earth
with love,
it is an act

of divine union.
We carry God
to her bosom.
We find God
in her soul.

4th June, 1984.

DEAF GOD

I am suddenly angry with God!
I've been thinking of the streets
and all its misery and degradation,
thinking of our faith,
and our hope,
thinking of God's promise -
to heal, transform,
listen to her people...
and I wondered,
perhaps,
if God had gone
a little deaf
of late?
Wondered
why she did not
answer,
when her people
believed and called.
I told her she was slow,
and needed, perhaps,
to get moving,
to answer her people!

I thought about
the daughter of Jairus,
the centurion's servant,
and countless other miracles
and wondered,
is God asleep?

I got God in a corner,
and told her
what I thought of her.
No wonder the powers of darkness
rage and gather!
Answer!
Mighty God!

Answer,
Mother God!
Listen to your faithful few
who are daft enough
to believe in
the Promise of
the Kingdom,
and to believe
that it must
be now,
can be now.

Where are your friends
Mighty God?
Where your glory, and power
to scatter, and destroy
the evil, the darkness,
the poverty
in which we walk?
Where is your promise,
Oh God?
Don't let those who
despise you,
and those who

scoff,
trample your Kingdom,
in the garbage and mud
of the city streets.
Don't stand by,
and watch death laugh.
Don't look on,
and see your children
crumple,
and fall
before the darkness.

Hey! Mighty God -
rise up,
stir yourself!
Our
"I believe"
should be enough
to send darkness
screaming
and death howling.
Should be enough
to establish
the Kingdom
in Pigeon Square,
and outside the bar,
on Broadway.

Ah,
We have to
feel God in our lives.
We have to
run with him,
sleep with her,
eat with her,
cry with him....
It is the Great Reckoning,
the mindless, passionate
rendezvous,

during which we
can say to the Creator,
"Dammit! - what are you up to?"
And still know
that we will end up together,
rolling and laughing
on the forest floor.

Yes,
We have within us
the given power
to make God stir, and
the whole court of heaven
rise, startled,
to hear us.

5th June, 1984. Yorkville.

I have often been bored and restless during days of solitude in the forest, and, at the same time, experienced a quality and a richness that by far compensate for the dry, empty times. It must be that both have to exist together, like a spider's web.

It is not in human nature to be continually aware of the joy and grace of God. I have to simply be, boredom, listlessness and all, always expectant and prepared to sit out the long, long wait. God never fails, though admittedly, She is often a little slow.

I am here now, and I listen to the faint stirring of the leaves, the occasional barking of a dog in the far distance, the sense of utter
- peace
- simplicity
- stillness.....

This sacred time is rare and very, very beautiful. The candle flame is still. Reminds me of the Sahara Desert, where I spent three months in solitude and prayer, just a few years ago. I thank God for this blessed time. I am convinced that all times of solitude given to God, bear fruit when least expected. Perhaps, I will never see the fruit, but I have been called for the sowing of the seed. I, like the seed which is sowed, must die before bearing fruit. Death, is a time of great celebration, when we have discovered the meaning of life which leads us to rejoicing in death. Death is a new life.

....and don't I pray for the Kingdom? Ah, I pray a lot for the Kingdom. I give the pearl of great price for it. I give my life for it. What else makes sense?

10th June, 1984. Chicago.

Dolores is in hospital. This is where we began, in hospital, eighteen months ago. She looks as bad now as she did then. I grieve for her and for my own helplessness. But I believe she will live. God holds her. Still it is very hard. We didn't visit her until the fourth day. We want her to understand that we want nothing to do with her wilful dying, only with her choosing to live. We walk on the knife edge of life and death with Dolores......
God - God - God - God!
Death only makes sense when it comes out of choosing life.

14th June, 1984.

I went out today visiting the bars. I met Kitty. She is bound by despair and utter sadness, a woman deeply hurt and abused, drinking away her pain in the bar every night.

I also met Linda, the bartender. Linda is buxom, blonde always waiting for her truck driver lover to come. Tonight she was laughing and looked lovely. She is a warm and good hearted woman. But she is so afraid! Will he come tonight? Will he ever come back?

There was Edward, who digs graves and will retire in November. He is full of bonhomie and loneliness, drinking every night, a long slow drunk, hoping for a quick and quiet death.

16th June, 1984.

DID I SEE YOU?

Did I See You, God?
On the Broadway,
where dirty garbage and broken glass
is kicked about and
scattered around
the greasy sidewalk,
I thought I smelled God.

In the bar,
with music shrieking,
air thick with tobacco haze, and
the stink of stale beer,
I thought I heard God.

In the brothel,
with its despairing waits
joyless jokes,
distorted sex and
verbal violence,
I thought I touched God.

In the soup kitchen,
where sick and lonely people
shuffled in line for
plastic plates and orange juice.
I thought I saw God.

God, God.
Oh, did I really see you, God?
Where did I see you, God?

22nd June, 1984.

It has been very busy at May's. Rene and Lee are still working. May is still bitter and negative, but I don't know if it is my imagination or hope, she seems more subdued, somehow sadder.

Dolores is back in a transient hotel. I took her some of her clothes. She looks so sad, so sick, so humiliated. She didn't want me to see her room. Jeremy, her former pimp, is drunk in it. She looked completely crushed. I felt deeply for her, and inside me I felt a deep longing to do something, but I know I cannot do for her what she needs to do for herself. Only the grace of God is left now.

I left her and went to supper with Irene. Her stomach is swollen with her distended liver, but she refuses to believe it. She denies her choice of death, and only smiles pretending her hell will go away. At midnight, Brenda, a Canadian Indian who has been wandering around Chicago like a lost soul for a few months, came to Genesis House. She is only 21 and looks like an old lady. She should have been a splendid woman, not a poor image of one. We gave her a bed for the night and asked no more questions.

23rd June, 1984.

I was with Brenda most of today. After spending a small fortune on telephone calls, we eventually put her on a bus back to Canada. It cost us over $80.00 but we felt it was worth it to get her off these streets, where she would be a target for a pimp or for rape. She said thanks, but I am not sure she knew what was happening.

In the evening, I walked the streets and found Belinda in a tavern. She is a white "hill-billy", or so she seems to be known. Belinda is a rough, tough young lady, with a hard and vicious look. She was planning to shoot another woman. She has already served time for murder. Belinda said you had to be tough to survive on these streets, "You have to kill", she insists. I wonder if she ever knew real friendship, trust or love. Is that why there is so much anger and hate inside her? I left her at 2.00 a.m., finally convinced she will not kill tonight. How does one bring the Kingdom here, Lord? I am exhausted!

Pray! Believe! Pray!

"He will give strength to your bones and you shall be like a watered garden, like a spring of water whose waters never run dry." (Is 58:11)

28th June, 1984.

I went to a workshop on Gestalt Therapy and it was very good. I had to look at me, my weaknesses, my boundaries, who I am, and who I claim to be. I feel I have been torn apart and dessicated in the last few weeks with so many traumas, pains and fears. Sometimes my boundaries get blurred and I need to recognise and hold on to the truth, found within me, which tells me not to compromise or play games.

In this chaotic world of the streets, boundaries are murky, so unclear, as to hardly exist. Surrounded by violence and chaos it is often difficult not to be affected by it. There is so much manipulation and distortion on the streets I sometimes wonder what is reality and what is not. So many people I meet have been manipulated by family and society, and it is the only way they know how to relate. All of us can become addicted, and play games. in the midst of this I must remain who I am, protect the "me" which could be lost, burnt out. I must keep my soul from selling out, pretending I am the savior of these streets. I must believe in miracles, God's miracles.

Dolores called tonight, still sober, sensible, in contact. Oh God, give me a break - let this little bit of light and trembling hope turn out to be real. Let this one live. I must believe in the Kingdom, even if the lights are turned down very, very low.

1st July, 1984

WHOLENESS

Gather everything together
like the enveloping dusk.
Welcome it,
delight in it,
dreams and images,
memories,
hopes, pains -
Recall -
Relive -
Be-friend.
Let the past surge
forward into the gentle,
welcoming present, and
take each
far-wandered memory
into your bosom to kiss,
caress, and
claim your own,
your self.
Befriend,
reclaim your wholeness and
all the fragmented beauty of
who you are.

3rd July, 1984.

ASLEEP

Sometimes it is hard to pray,
I fall asleep
in God.
The deep silence,
the lovely simplicity of

this tiny room,
leaves me
like a child,
in a mother's arms.
I can only sleep.
But isn't that
the most beautiful, and true
picture of all -
the child asleep
in the mother's arms?
Silent.
Reborn.
Nurtured.

6th July, 1984.

Dolores hovers in the background of my mind, continually. I feel she is very near death and I am hanging in between the tension of hope and death - faith and reality. I have prayed so much for this one daughter of God. I have hammered heaven, wept, shouted, whispered, threatened, demanded, pleaded. Yes, I have done it all! And there goes Dolores, seemingly plunging towards death. I keep holding on, yet terrified to think how I might feel if she dies and turns her back on life and healing. It would be a great blow to the faith I have held onto all this time with Dolores - believing God will hold her up and transform her. God has choices, and from where I stand I would find it hard to understand if God did not choose to give Dolores the grace she needs for life. Or is it that God always gives the grace but can be rejected by us, rejected by Dolores? Is God stuck too? Is God mourning and grieving too? Can God do more? Can God do more than offer us infinite opportunities without interfering with human freedom?

"Oh Lord, are you as tired as I am? Don't give up! So many times Dolores said, *Don't give up on me*. You never will. I never have. I didn't give up on Dolores." There is to be no more approval or disappointment, no more blame or praise, no more plans or schemes for, or with, Dolores. Dolores is bruised enough! She must be free to die. It is perhaps that last dignity she can claim. Dolores has taught me that God is God. I must not fall into the temptation, we ministers face all the time, to play God. We can do nothing more than sit with the poverty and pain of the oppressed and marginalized people, and ask God's compassion and mercy for those of us who are blind and uncaring.

We need to sit in the streets and back alleys of our cities and towns, without power or consolation - with the sin we have created. Only thus may we find a way for any healing or reconciliation to occur. Only when we stand in the paradox that makes each one of us both oppressed and oppressor, both victim and perpetrator, do we really know love and compassion. If we honestly face our own strengths and weaknesses, we learn to see reality with a clarity that only comes from God. However, for those of us who fancy ourselves as catalysts of change, or active healing ministers, being a silent presence is an anguish.

Yet how dare I, in this place, be anything else? Salvation is already given. I always seem to be forgetting that...

RUN

Of course I want to run away
and yes,
of course I want to say, "Enough"
Yes - yes
of course
I am human
and very limited.
Who would ever want to be a saint?
Being human is hard enough -
Sometimes, I am sure,
it is not only good,
but necessary -
to run away
awhile.

Dolores: 23rd July, 1984 (Transient Hotel)

Dear Edwina, Just a few lines to tell you I was thinking of you right now, laying here on my back. For a moment I put all the bad and hurting times away. I layed them under my bed. We had beautiful times together, going places. Seeing things I never dreamed I would ever see. I hope one day I can start over again, where I stopped at. You made something, some one out of me. There is some I can still feel. The rest is frozen and I know it is up to me to thaw it. I think you have not gave up on me entirely. I feel a little hope left in me. Edwina I'm so concerned time is running out for me. Edwina nothing comes through my head. I want sobriety but for how long? That is what confuses me. I know there is not anything you can do. But be at my self. I need help, I'm praying, but praying tells me the same thing you tell me. Dolores can only do it - make her own decisions.

As you know I love you. Truly I do.

Dolores.

Dolores: 24th July, 1984. Yorkville.

I have not written in such a long time, and it is hard to know where to start. It has been about three months since I been on my drinking spree. I'm on last string of ropes. Ready to fall. Or have I? I been living in the dumps, hospital etc. My friends gave up on me. But they still love me. Why? Myself I have not gave up hope. I still have a little left in my little guts. I made an ass out of myself. "Oh, God!" What should I do? Drinking is my life. I choose it (Dolores). I enjoy drinking. My friends are right. I will never give up drinking. Yes, maybe just for a while I will give it up. If I had one wish, my wish would be, not to have an urge to drink anymore. Yes, I am scared to die. I don't want to die. Sometimes I wonder, how far am I really from death? I am so grateful that I have friends like the VMM. I am happy they took me in because I am sick. I myself don't think I would of made it alone. Right now I am living hour by hour and day by day. This is the worse I been. My legs are swollen. My eyes are jaundiced. I am weak.

I am free now. No more meetings. No program. No counselor. No half-way house. Is this free, or am I just punishing myself? Is this what I want? Yes? No? Right now I am a little confused so I will write a little tomorrow night.

As you read you can see my mind is not too much working.

Dolores.

Dolores: 25th July, 1984.

I'm no use to anything or anybody anymore. I have no one to blame but me. "Damn it!" I'm so messed up, confused. I can not cry anymore. I hit the bottom so low in the ground, that I can not get up off the ground. Because I'm so low down in it. And I don't feel sorry for myself because I put myself there. This is all I can write today about myself. Maybe tomorrow my life is gone. There is no use but I still think there's hope left somewhere, somehow.

Dolores and Teddy Bear.

Dolores: 26th July, 1984.

Still here and alive. Today I was not in good spirits. Not happy at all, why? Big question. Edwina came to visit. The evening was great but I was not. I must pull myself together. Life could not be that bad. I have everything right in front of me. Am I scared of what will become of it? I should not because VMM don't expect anything. They gave up on all my expectations. I will try harder. I felt alone knowing I was not. Strange feeling! I want to reach out to someone. But afraid, I don't want to hurt anyone anymore.

Maybe. No, it is O.K. I will work something out.

Thank you, Lord, for this day. I am very grateful for this day.

Dolores and Teddy Bear.

Dolores: 2nd August, 1984.

Still sick (a little). They been great, Yorkville has. They make me feel good about myself. Specially Edwina and Maria. But! I know I will be going soon. Back to Uptown. Why? I'm a little worried about my stomach. I have these lumps around my navel and I keep swelling up all over. Anyways I'm wondering am I really happy? How could I when my life is so sick and confused? I had a chance of going to Chicago today but did not. I wish I was normal. Anyways I hope I sleep through the night.

Dolores.

5th August, 1984.

BALANCE

So much struggling -
realising that I need a balance
between reaching out and reaching in.
I need to do some things just for me,
like paint and play,
and read and build sandcastles.
I need to stop
for a long time,
to think about that.
Where did I miss it? Lost it?
For joy is the center of ministry.
Joy should precede ministry,
nurture it and fulfill it.
But I am so intense about ministry,
and take it so solemnly
(as if I were responsible for it)
that I become weighed down
by its ups and downs,
its disappointments and failures.
I suffocate joy with
seriousness....

I imagine everything depends on me -
when everything is God's business,
and God has already taken care of
all her creation
and all her people.
We are only to walk with each other
be with each other,
love each other,
God's is the healing,
the growing,
and the fulfilling.
When I lose perspective
and imagine everything,
(or most things)
revolving around myself,
I make myself
a little god,
and lose my joy.
For I was never made
to be a little god - only
to be loved
by the Great God.
Perhaps I am too busy
trying to love other people
instead of learning
to love myself.
When I can do that
I might begin to understand
how great God's love is.
When I go thru'
darkness, heaviness and anxiety,
it is God's invitation
for me to stop
looking outwards
and start
looking inwards
and be loving and gentle
with myself.
I am called to minister

for my own joy.
When my joy diminishes,
so does my ministry.
When I have fun and
enjoy myself
God does!
Then I am most like God -
who is joy!

13th August, 1984. Yorkville.

GOD'S WISDOM

I have never seen so many wild flowers -
purple, white, yellow,
rising and falling,
swaying and dancing,
with God, whilst
the warm breeze hums,
and all, all of it,
is drenched in
rare sweet perfume.
Ah, God's breath!
"Show me your wisdom, Lord",
I prayed.
"This", said the Lord,
"is my wisdom."
And all around stretched
the great field of wild flowers
and glorious weeds
of all colors
and heights and variety.
The breeze gently rocked them,
bees, flies and colored butterflies
hovered, then burrowed
into the hearts
of the chosen flowers,

providing life and nurturing,
even to the little ones.
Tho' all so different,
together the mass of flowers
were splendid
in their variety.
But each alone was beautiful
and unique and stood proud,
sharing equally with all the others,
the loving breeze and
the warm sun.
In the wildness, in the freedom,
was splendid harmony,
and, from it all,
a glorious perfume rose,
as God breathed and danced
amongst Her flowers.
"This", whispered the Perfume,
"is my wisdom."

15th August, 1984.

AWARE

Mary stands at the cross,
compassionate woman, waiting
for the death of Jesus.
She is simply there,
waiting, waiting for the death
grieving,
present,
- aware.
We compassionate women
cannot resurrect or heal,
cannot even console.
The dying Christ
is beyond consolation or healing,

He is simply dying.
The compassionate woman
knows that, and waits.
She has embraced the death.
We embrace the death.

18th August, 1984.   Chicago.

HELL'S STREETS

Out walking after midnight -
sad, lonely people
shuffling along the filthy streets,
strewn with garbage.
Eskimo Joe - with tears
in his eyes - caught unawares -
looking for a bush to sleep under.
Janice with her bag of french fries
hurrying off the station steps
to sleep fitfully.
Jim - wandering with his
canvas bag slung around him,
face contorted with tears
flowing freely.
The heavy black woman shouting
on the corner, and I,
we stopped and talked awhile.

She was filled with anger,
resentment, pain -
we are white -
we are rich -
she, alienated, desperate.
She too, cannot fight the tears.
Ah, four weeping adults
in the morning hours
among the garbage.

The little lady, hardly fourteen,
being dragged along,
staggering, in red hot pants
by a black pimp -
abused, drugged,
a child -
who should be clutching a doll,
not a pimp.

Johnny and his pals
drinking wine on the church steps,
looking for jobs and places to stay.

Broken lonely people
on Hell's Streets.
God?

22nd August, 1984

I spent some time at May's today.

Lee showed me her family photos. I saw her young, girlish, innocent, until her step-father molested her. The more recent photos were filled with sexual innuendos, like the one where she is half naked with Vernon, her man. The contrast between the smiling, child-like family photos and the more recent ones is terrible. The transformation created by the violence of rape and incest on a young, young child.

Bob, whom the girls call a freak and a wierdo, told me his mother died when he was six years old. He was in care until he was seventeen, and then the seminary and priesthood. He never forgave his mother for dying. Now...well, he comes to the brothel whenever he can, in spite of a wife and a grown-up family. This is a sad, brutal place - I feel exhausted after just half a day. Lee was talking about buying herself a pistol.

Yesterday, I took Irene, Eskimo Joe and Ann to Yorkville for the day. They loved it. Joe, as usual, was silent and deeply sad, a hurting man. We got back at 11.00 p.m and Joe slept in the basement of Genesis House. It is these moments when people can put aside their fears and play, which give meaning to all I am trying to do here. The majority of people in the streets, never had a childhood, in which they were allowed to play. Their lives have always been a very serious, life or death, affair. How do I teach a grown man to play?

We are now three in our little community at Genesis House! Judy (whom I spent a year with at theology school) came to join us. Her skills in counselling and listening will be a great help for our chaotic and troubled population. Welcome Judy!

4th September, 1984

ALIVE

In the hermitage in Yorkville overnight...
all I can hear are millions of crickets and cicadae
like a great chorus all around me.
Oh, it is so beautiful!
So rich in a sense of
peace and well being.
Here, I am aware of myself
fully alive and present,
alert to all the beauty,
of the forest at night.
I feel blessed here - one here.
It is all so simple, so silent, so alone.
Here there is energy, awareness.
Oh! I feel so alive!
My soul it is that dances.

This evening I saw
two butterflies in love.
This evening I knew also,

that Dolores is dying,
slowly in her hole,
in the transient hotel.
Let God do all.

10th September, 1984.

AMERICA THE BEAUTIFUL

America the beautiful -
salute the flag,
while down the dirty alley
old ladies scavenge for
cans and garbage scraps.
And Mick, bent and broken,
shuffles down the street,
picking up the fag ends,
center of his life.

America the beautiful -
salute the flag,
while the lines
at the soup kitchen,
all ragged and shamed,
grow longer and longer
in winter's cold dusk.

America the beautiful -
salute the flag,
and in the darkened hallways
the old folks huddle
under yesterday's papers
claiming a stronger,
rising dollar.

America the beautiful -
salute the flag,

and raise it in the shelters
where the weak and hungry
in their dirty, smelly clothes,
are too sick,
too old,
too poor,
to raise the flag themselves.
America the beautiful -
Ah, bury, bury your flag,
until the smallest of your children
can raise it up themselves.

Dolores: 14th September, 1984.

Here I go again in the hospital. This time it is my foot. I have to have surgery and believe me I'm scared. But they will put me to sleep. I just pray that my liver will take it. I've been here since last night. I did not get a bed until after 11.00 p.m. It took twelve hours. I am so hungry and thirsty.

O Dear Lord, I am so frightened. Please help me through this pain and surgery. I want to live. I want to make it through this world.

Dear Dolores/Teddy Bear,

What are you feeling now? I know what you are feeling. You're ready to run. But is this what we want? We have nothing so why not go? But are we ready or even strong enough? We know we don't want to die. We are scared. We can not stay here forever. So we better go before we get too attached or too close to the ones we love. Just let feelings stay where they're at. No further. We can't afford it or I don't think they can either. So the time is now. Are we ready? You know what that means for us. We will take life one day at a time or even day and night at a time.

Love you,
Dolores/Teddy Bear.

Dolores: 15th September, 1984.

Oh, God, what am I going to do with my life (my drinking problem)? What? I don't know. I know I want to live a decent life. My drinking sickness is the main issue. To be truthful I do not know if I really want to stop. But will it mean I lost everything. I lost anyway. But I could win the battle. And believe me, it is a hard one. I know I tried before. My feeling is, "Yes, I am hurt." When will I wake up and see the light?
Love,
        Dolores.

21st September, 1984. Yorkville.

SILENT SONG

Did you bring me here
to challenge, to fight,
to demonstrate, to discuss?

Did you bring me here,
to listen, to debate,
to consider, to plead?

Ah -
Am I here
because this is my life blood
and I cannot live without
the Silent Confrontation?

No. No words here.
No reflections or discussions,
no sad, sad case or broken life.
Just the constant harmony
of the host of crickets humming
unceasingly all around me
in the damp brown earth.

That, yes, that
is wisdom and harmony enough.
Ah - how I miss the crickets!

I can hear a bird - just one
among the crickets, filling the night air.
But my song is silent.

God isn't singing tonight either.

I wish I could take all this beauty
into my heart,
soak it up, absorb it -
the riotous colors and the endless song
of birds and crickets,
then, perhaps, I too,
would be filled with color,
and sing an endless song.

Dolores: 24th September, 1984.

One week and five days I been here at hospital. My surgery went good. Very painful after the surgery. The doctor put another cast on my foot/leg. I don't feel too much pain now. Just now and then I do. I have a decision to make. Stay sober or stay a drunk. I know I need to make it. I need some help. Judy been here today. Brought me a transistor radio to use while I'm here. They all been great to me since I been in hospital. I love it. I'm so grateful that I know them. Sometimes I wonder to myself, do I deserve to have someone like them (Edwina, Judy, Ted, Su, Maria, VMM)? They are a gift from God and it is the best gift I have ever received and it is a blessing.

Dolores: 28th September, 1984

I feel very alone. No one has come to see me. They are probably busy doing their work.

Dolores: 29th September, 1984.

Two weeks I been here. It is no pleasure, believe me. I feel so lonely. Not depressed but lonely. The cast is very uncomfortable. It's a matter of days till I'm discharged and I have not made any decisions yet. I feel great about being sober. If I would not have broken my ankle would I have been sober? To be honest, I don't think so. I really believe I needed my ankle to get broken to get myself together. To rest and think. When each day comes I get more scared because the day is just around the corner. Just like A.A. taught me, one day at a time. The reason I'm frightened is because I don't know what is happening next because I know what I am capable of doing. I don't want to hurt and nor hurt anyone else.

Alcoholic	I am a alcoholic
Boring	There is a lot of time when I feel boring
Confused	I'm so confused most of the time
Daring	I do a lot of crazy, daring things
Endless	Sometimes I feel my life is endless
Frightened	I am frightened of what my life is about
Goofy	I do many goofy things at times
Health	My health is very sick
Insecure	I'm insecure when I don't have my teddy with me
Journal	I write in a journal when something bothers me
Kicks	I get my kicks by drinking sometimes
Loving	I have many loving friends that care
Moody	I am a moody person

Neutral	I'm not neutral at this moment
Oppose	There are situations when I oppose
Principal	The principal of me being here is my foot
Quit	I must quit drinking
Restless	I feel restless in hospital
Scared	I'm scared of death
Together	One day I will be together
Understand	
V	
Wrong	I always do the wrong thing

I will make it one day. I must. Before something dread-ful happens.
> Love,
>> Dolores.

30th September, 1984.

It is almost winter - makes me huddle up inside myself and reminisce about tea and crumpets and a coal-fire in Lancashire when I was a child.

Tammy is with us, young, violent, difficult, but very much a child beneath it all.

Dolores: 3rd October, 1984.

Bored. Bored. Talked to Edwina. I think for sure I will be discharged in the morning. I'm going to start some hobbies and try my best helping as much as I can possibly do. I think that's what I am going to do. I feel this is my last hope to find where I am going from here.

Dear God,

Thank you for the day. Thank you for the food that makes me strong. Please God let me be strong. Help me through these weeks while I am in this foot cast and I thank Su and VMM helping me through this for letting me stay with them and so beautiful. Well like I said before can't blame nobody but myself.

    Love,

      Dolores.

6th October, 1984.

It's been a crazy week! Dolores is still in hospital. Tammy has been off three times on all-night binges. All around me is violence, anger and hurt! Tammy is wild, hurting, vicious. Like all the others, she was once a child, innocent and hopeful, until her grandfather raped her at 6 - or 7 - or 8 years. She hit the streets at 9 years of age and has been there ever since. What can we do for the Tammys? How do you heal such violence inflicted on children? They spend their lives self-destructing. So many of us kid ourselves saying it is not our responsibility. "I have never hit anyone!" "I have never raped or stolen, I have only minded my own business!" and so on and on. But let's stop lying to ourselves. We commit those crimes on children when we close our eyes and our ears to what is going on. We become the oppressors when we neglect to speak out for the hurt children of our world. We rape when we gather more around ourselves than we could possibly need, leaving others scraping for survival. We are one society, one world, infinitely involved in each other's survival. We are our brothers' and sisters' keepers! When we fail them, we fail ourselves.

7th October, 1984

Irene came over to visit in hysterics and on the edge of a nervous breakdown. Johnny followed her to the house, and they spent a little time together. It was filled with harshness and hurt. We ended up taking Irene to hospital for an alcoholic program. Dolores plods on passively and heavily in Yorkville - stuck because of her broken ankle - split by Jeremy with a baseball bat, in a fit of fury. Now Dolores clings to her hopelessness and lethargy. My heart sinks to witness her lack of effort. As soon as she can walk, she will hit the streets again - and again. I must stand and watch. How hard that is!

We have another woman with us tonight - Ernestine, 43, black, unemployed - trying to make it on $144.00 per month. So many of the women want to destroy themselves. Life, it seems, is unendurable for them. I think I am beginning to understand.

8th October, 1984

Irene walked out of her alcohol program after only two days.

Dolores: 8/9 October, 1984 (1.00 a.m.)

Had a good day but a very confused one (Naturally!) I felt early today that I wanted to go back to the streets (drinking!). I wanted to talk to Su but I did not know how, so it got late. It came to me again. I wanted to tell someone, anyone. But it wasn't the time or place at the end. I kinda told Edwina. I know I hurted her but did not mean to.

Oh Lord, what's wrong with me, here I am with a broken foot and I, Dolores, with a half dead liver, wants to go back to the streets. What is it with me? Am I such a horrible monster that likes to do these terrible things?

Why can I not be like normal persons, and choose the good instead of the bad things?

9th October, 1984 (written by Edwina in Dolores' journal)

Dear Monster,

You can do anything you choose to do - however long it takes.
    Love,
        Edwina.

Dolores: 9th October, 1984

11.30 p.m. Miserable Tuesday.

Can I really choose even as long as it takes? Could I really believe that? I was really angry today. I wanted to go back to Chicago but Edwina would not drive me. I know she done it for my own good. Do people understand that I'm a loser, failure with little hope? Maybe I don't want to make it in life. I choose it, and sit in my own shit. "Oh, but I do understand how they feel." They want Dolores, to see Dolores make it. But the point is, do I, Dolores, want to see her make it or go down to shit? At this point I don't know what to do. What can I do? I'm stuck. Broken foot. Maybe I'm just being thick headed about it all. Should I give myself a chance? What possibly can I do with one foot? So Dolores, don't be stupid. Just wait, things might get better. Can it get worse?

I wonder at times how long it will take, after my cast is off to be back on the streets? One, two days or a week? Matter of hours maybe? Or will a miracle happen and I stick to sobriety?

Dolores: 13th October, 1984

I feel to be alone. So here I am sitting in Edwina's room all alone. Watching the little portable T.V. I just feel to be alone today. I'm not bored because there is always something here for me to do. Maybe a little depressed. Woke up feeling bad. How I wish I was in Chicago - don't know how long I can make it.

Dear God,

Help me through my struggles in my life. It's very hard for me. I'm hurting and don't know which way to look, turn or go. It is like a road and don't know what exit to get off at.
    Love,
        Dolores.

Dolores: 14th October, 1984

Well, I have not found any exit or any stop signs. But my day was pleasant. Judy came. We went out to a movie and dinner. Was very good to get out. Was good, Judy is such a beautiful person. We had a nice time together, matter of fact it was our first time together out. I must admit it does feel good to be sober and not hung-over. Sometimes I think laying here where and why or when did I go wrong at or even that first mistake. Sometimes I think or wish I can make a rerun of my life and see where I had made that terrible step. But I know it will be painful to even look back.

Dear Dolores,

I think you're doing great. I am very astonished and happy that you are sober. But ....how long will it last? Another week or matter of days. I am very concerned about your abilities and health. Just want to let you know I care and love you deeply in my heart.
    Love,
        Your Inner Feeling.

15th October, 1984. (Entry by Edwina in Dolores' journal)

Dear Noodle Head,

I am delighted that you are sober - you always look great when you are sober, you even sound intelligent!

However, I know there is a lot of denial and pretense going on in you, i.e. the streets are great, the streets are exciting, my life on the streets was good....Yorkville is dull and boring, there is no fun etc. etc. This is a whole bunch of lies which you keep treating yourself to in order to fool yourself and live in a pretend world that is not wonderful and exciting at all but instead is dirty, painful and shitty.

But - you are old enough - and you know enough. You also know the truth and you will never be able to cover that up completely or fool yourself completely. One day you might start taking life and yourself seriously instead of playing games. I still pray for that day before it is too late (and don't fool yourself on that one either - you won't last long on the streets). I love you, Dolores - I always will, even if you ruin what is left of your life...You know the options. You know you have choices.

We love you,
       Edwina.

Dolores: 16th October, 1984

The day was a strange one. I have the biggest choice to make by tomorrow night. Go back to Chicago or stay here. I know what I should do but the point is, do I want to? I know in the future I will regret it but I know I will be too late. I already know what I will do and I'm scared. Oh, why am I so hard, thick headed? I really don't know why I should be scared because I made it on the streets. I might have been unhappy. "Maybe I did not know what un-happy was?"

HELP!

I am getting older, not younger. Dumber, not wiser either.

Dolores: 17th October, 1984

My last night to make my decisions. Well I have not yet. But I have the feeling what the answer is and am sorry. Sorry for the people I'm hurting and myself.

What am I going to do or go? I am scared. So why am I going and do I realize what I'm doing? I am sick. Very ill. I want to run right now. How can I face Su in the morning when I tell her what I decided or even say it to Edwina on the phone? I can feel this is my last time. If I go I can not return or stay.

Dolores: 18th October, 1984 - County Clinic, Chicago.

Here I am sitting waiting. I'm early and I have a little patience. Am all alone now. Su dropped me off. Going back to the streets. That was my decision. So here I sit with a broken foot, don't know what next. I feel sad because this is not what I really want. How can I be so stupid and do this to myself? I brought this notepaper with me so I can remember and keep up my feelings.

Dolores: 18th October, 1984 - Transient Hotel.

Here I am again. Well things are not so good. Edwina just called. Happy to hear that she still loves me and cares. I feel hungry. I must admit I am drinking wine. Someone came by and brought me a quart so I drank it. So now I am going outside. Stupid I know.

Dolores: 19th October, 1984

Still here. Staying with Calvin and I shot some drugs. Feel good but still feel a bit sad. Calvin is nice. He won't take advantage of me. But....keep me high. Calvin is out doing his business. I am not hungry, but sure is cold. It is cold outside. If I get enough to drink I will try to get outside and make some money. My foot is in pain because of the dampness and rain. Maybe things will pick up later.

Dolores: 21st October, 1984

I feel like a prisoner as I usually do. I must admit it's me doing this. I am alone and going crazy. What is wrong? I had not a shot of dope and wine since 11.00 this morning, escaping is what I am doing. Yes, they are right. I can escape. But when I wake up it is still there, never leaves, or even gets worse.

But why do I refuse to give up?

I feel hungry. Maybe someone will come through, never know! I am mostly alone here so I try to think, but I just dream. Good dreams like walking, laughing, being someone that does not live in a fantasy life. I think I will rest now. Perhaps take a hop around the block. How I wish I did not have this cast.

Thank you, God, for this day. For being alive. Even for the rain.

Dolores: 23rd October, 1984. Afternoon.

The day is not so good. I been high. But not drinking so much. It's cold. My foot is getting along pretty good. I ate today - some eggs. I have to try to do something. I have no money. There is a TV here so it is keeping me occupied. So I don't feel so lonely.

3.20 p.m.

Still Tuesday, I feel pretty good about myself now. I just took a wash up, change my blouse. I cleaned the room. My foot feels much better. Got high again. Calvin been so good to me. He is not like the other guys. He does not ask for any sex. We even sleep together. Maybe tomorrow I will try to get out for some groceries at one of the pantries. I feel I should try to do something than sit on my ass. We do need food. Anyway, I should try to do something to contribute something for me staying here because I am eating and sleeping in Calvin's home.

11.15 p.m.

I had a good day. I been getting along since my foot is O.K. I been up around. But! I am escaping. I been high all day. I did a lot of drugs. I need to get some clothes from the Salvation Army. I'm thinking about getting back on Public Aid since my life have changed so brutally.

What can I say except thank the Lord for this day and my thanks for keeping me from all danger.

Dolores: 31st October, 1984

Dear Edwina, Judy & Ted,

Just a few lines to say hello and to thank you all for tolerating me. As you know I am hard headed. There are times when I am alone, I wonder why I do stupid things to myself knowing that it is wrong. And yes, I know that I can do something about it. To tell the truth, I am scared. Why, I don't know. Maybe it is sobriety that is because I am escaping reality, but I have not been drinking a lot. But I have been involved with drugs. My foot is driving me crazy. I know that my foot is not O.K. I am not happy at all. I hurts myself so I must face the truth. I am so grateful for having friends like you.

You are the best people that I ever had in my entire life. Because you are beautiful people I think of you very often. I don't like the way I am living, or doing. I can not blame nobody but myself. There are times when I am alone, I look, stare at the walls. I don't cry all the time but I do a lot. I know this might sound like I am feeling sorry for myself but this is how I feel inside. I also feel like I am going crazy. I still have a lot of confusion, maybe more than I think. I need help bad. I know what I should do about it, but I am afraid. I need a rest. I am so tired and fed up to the point I can not think or sleep. At least I am not sleeping right. I would like to maybe come over to visit you all if it is O.K. with you all, when you're not busy. If it is alright with you three. I love you all and I thank you Edwina for trusting me.

I don't know what to do so I am asking you to help me please. I will co-operate also. I think I am finally giving up because I know it is about that time because I can not cope with it anymore. Is it that I am tired of it all? I can not make it too far because I am weak but I know I must not give up. The real reason I wrote was because I had to let someone know how I feel and you are the only people that I can depend and also understand. I know I could of telephoned but I would not say the words I really wanted to say. Anyways you know I'm just noodled headed. I know I tell you I am O.K. but I really is not. You probably know. I try to talk to my Higher Power for help, believe me I do. But nothing seems to happen. So I am still trying. I have not given up on my Higher Power because I know I will reach my Higher Power one day. I still have faith and hope within myself.

So I am asking you all to say a prayer for me. Need all I can get. So I will close this letter with all my heart and love, O.K. Specially a lot of kisses and hugs. Excuse the handwriting and the mistakes that because I am under a lot of stress right now, this minute.

Love you forever,
Dolores.

2nd November, 1984.

In the hermitage....

TIME TO BE

The leaf.....
when it has given of its first beauty
mellows and is rich in its maturity,
delights the eye when it falls to the earth.
It returns to the place from which it came,
swallowed and consumed by mother earth,
to provide life to the new leaves.
We all go back to the earth,
part of the cycle of death
and resurrection.
The richer the soil,
the healthier the new leaves.

It is important to spend time like this,
without urgency or action,
just being here present,
enjoying being.
Time and leisure enough to savor

a leaf falling,
a spider crawling,
to hear the wood crackle,
the wind whisper,
to be fully and wondrously aware
of being alive.
Ah, that is my special joy -
to be alive, to truly,
deeply know it,
and treasure it.

To do so, we must not only
be conscious of the myriad
forms of life around us,
we have also to be in relationship with them.
We do not live in isolation
from all the life which God created
in the world.
We would be diminished
and wounded.

So, when the earth is abused and raped -
so are we.
When anything is wantonly killed or hurt,
something in us is too -
our harmony with God's creation, destroyed.
To be so interrelated
can give the greatest you
and the greatest pain.

Ah, I am in love with the forest!

3rd November, 1984.

PRESENCE

God is present
in the wood stove and the oil lamp,
in the gathering shadows
and the silent stars.
If she does not seem present
in my heart and soul -
it is because I have limited God too much.

Perhaps I should listen more intently
to the wood crackling,
and watch more closely,
the oil wick flicker,
to allow God's presence
to envelop me.

Can I rediscover God's glory
in what appears to be
trivial and insignificant?

Thank you, God, for the blessed days,
I didn't do anything -
just wandered the forest,
struck dumb by the strength
of your trees and the
rich beauty of your dying leaves;
I sat by the stream and listened
to the murmur of your waters
and watched the rapid and lovely movements
of the squirrel among the branches;
I stood at night, awed by the vastness
of your sky
and the clear sharpness
of a hundred stars

and felt very, very small,
yet part of it all.
Thank you
God, for these days
when I walked in your Kingdom
and knew it.

More and more I think,
we look for God
in the wrong places.

It would probably be better
if we didn't look at all.

So busy looking,
we don't notice.
When it seems that God
slips quietly away,
and we sit sad and doubtful,
waiting, still hopeful,
we should smile and know
God is too near,
too deep to be noticed,
too close to be held,
She possesses us so
She runs through our veins,
breathing in our breath,
and beating in our hearts.
Ah, yes, when it seems that God
slips quietly away, we should
whisper our welcome
and know we are one.
God -
beating and breathing,
deep in our guts.

7th November, 1984. Chicago.

Tamika, who had stayed two months with us, left us for Minneapolis. We enjoyed her being here and are sad to see her go. She is not ready to face the world yet. This ministry is full of disappointments. But I know it has been good that she has been here and has experienced real love and caring. That surely must make a difference and be remembered. It is perhaps enough for now. Irene is staying with us - sick and weary with no purpose or aim in life. Dolores is deteriorating - now into drugs, very sick and confused. Ah, what awful destruction!

My spirits remain high, I feel confident in being here and I feel blessed in the midst of it all. God is with us - even if we are all broken up. We so often suck the human side out of our ministry, expecting the poor, the bruised, the broken to change their lives at the sound of Jesus' name. So many who encounter Jesus are too sick and hurting to have the energy or the hope to be open to transformation. I wonder if Jesus looked with love upon the prostitutes who stayed on the streets, the homeless, the poor and the handicapped and wished they could accept his love, whilst knowing they could not. I wonder if he also knew that, even in the most imperceptible of ways, love would change them forever.

Dolores: 7th November, 1984

Today I'm alright. This weekend and week I stayed high with drugs and alcohol. I been so mix up I can not think right. My memory is bad. I forget what I do.

This weekend I been in Uptown. Slept in the Shelter twice. I stayed at Edwina's place one night. I was ready to give up and go to the hospital but I was scared. I should have but I felt bad to go.

I wonder what is wrong with me? Why?
                    Dolores.

8th November, 1984.

In Genesis House tonight there were: Three prostitutes, two priests, Judy, who is a Religious sister, myself, Ted, a Religious Brother, and a pimp. After dinner we all went down to the basement chapel and prayed together. It was very special, very blessed.

We sat on the floor in a circle - prostitutes and priests, pimps and sister, lay and religious, black and white. I knew in an instant that this is what the Kingdom is all about - a bringing together of people who would never normally come together, a reaching out in silence and quiet pain to one another.

"The wolf and the young lamb will feed together, the lion eat straw like the ox - they will do no hurts, no harm on all my holy mountain, says Yahweh."   (Is 65: 25)

In those moments together we lived the Kingdom.

16th November, 1984

Debbie came to us for help. Her pimp had split her head in two great slashes. She had 78 stitches.

Dolores is back in hospital after Judy and I took her from the hotel and bathed her - she stank!

Lee, Irene and Tammy are in and out, feeling vey much at home here, which is good. But we are faced with so many questions and contradictions - Irene is staying here at the moment and, we suspect, still working in the brothel.

What is Genesis House? Is it a home for women who want to leave prostitution? Or can we also welcome those who are yet too afraid or insecure to have made a decision to change their lifestyles? Dare we take the risk of not laying down all the rules according to our own neat and ordered categories? Dare we be honest enough to embrace the reality of a little chaos?

If we want to welcome all, we cannot allow ourselves to play games. We cannot pretend we don't know a woman is working, otherwise the so-called healthy relationships with the women would be nothing but a farce. Is there a place where women who are still working can *be* without discrimination, pressure or expectation? What are our boundaries? We have to work out where we stand and be clear, in our words and our actions. These women have received too many double messages in their lives, they don't need it from us.

It is getting cold. The street people shiver in apprehension and pull their shabby coats tight around them. All of us fear the cold, which brings more misery to those already enduring too much.

THE PICNIC

They sat on the church's stone steps,
right on the corner where four roads meet
while anxious traffic sped and hooted past,
five middle-aged women dressed in assorted
mis-matched clothes and over-sized shoes.
Parked on the sidewalk, within easy reach,
stood their supermarket trolleys,
piled high with paper, bottles and beloved garbage.

The women, oblivious to the roar of the traffic,
did not care it was now the early hours
of the morning, and everyone was rushing home
to bed and shelter.

With loving, fastidious care,
they placed a tall plastic bottle of ginger ale
on the center step - and around it
five plastic cartons, collected in the day,
and washed in McDonald's restrooms.
Then, with self satisfaction and decorum,
they poured out the ale into the cartons.
"Half full for everybody", one said.

The ale was passed around.
The ladies grasped it
and supped the special treat -
trophy of the day's hunting.

Then followed a dozen compliments
on the quality and the sparkle
of the night's ale.

A few jokes, light hearted comments -
The darkness grew thicker,
the traffic lulled,
and, cradling the plastic cartons,
sensing the growing cold,
and the utter loneliness
of the empty bottle,
a terrible sadness took possession of
the five middle-aged ladies,
partners of the night,
and from their heaving souls broke out
a mighty silent scream.

17th November, 1984

Dolores is back with us from hospital - for how long? Will she ever believe she can try again? Lee came for supper. Irene is back. Well, we are all broken up, one way or another.

19th November, 1984

This has to be one of the craziest days!
Dolores was moody all day. Tammy was all jubilant about a new job with "big bucks" in a massage parlor, and she was elated and proud, a chance to start again. Irene went out all day with "old man Dave" and came back with Johnny, high on drugs and had a fight in the house. Tammy visited and stayed late. Mark (Gypsy) is here. Lee came also in the evening. That's ten folks in the house at one time or another today.

I went to the shelter tonight, and lo and behold, there was Tammy! The job she was so exalted about was a "con" - the guy was a pimp looking for women. She is hurt and dejected, but tries to cover.

Dolores: 20th November, 1984 - Genesis House.

I been off drugs and drinks for a week. I been in the hosp. since Sat. I stayed there for a few days. I have my cast off now. Just a bandage. Also I am at Genesis and doing good. I feel very happy. I feel good about being here, no negative feelings at all. I have not felt this good in months. I been here for three days and have not been bored at all. I do my best around. Irene and I share the third floor. We get along very good. Anyways, I'm happy and very grateful that they accept me here.

     Dolores.

24th November, 1984

We are laden with food baskets as Thanksgiving gifts from churches in the surburbs....we even have two turkeys. People are good, generous in spite of all the greed and violence in our world, Our cup runs over......

Dolores: 25th November, 1984

I am happy to be back at Genesis House. But the only thing that bothers me at times is where I am going from here. I kinda hope I don't have to ever go from here. I love being here. I do anything to stay here permanently. It has always been my dream to be here but I was too dumb to do the right thing at the beginning before I screwed up. Now I hope that day never comes that I have to leave Genesis House. I have got to love this house. I always did.

My Lord,
Thank you for this beautiful weekend. Also specially for being alive this day and night.
     Love,
      Dolores.

Dolores: 26th November, 1984.

I feel like a new person right now. Just being sober and living (staying) here at Genesis House. I don't never want to change. If I can do it and keep being straight with myself.

Dolores: 27th November, 1984.

I drank and I am sorry. Anyways I am scared because I don't want to be put out of Genesis House. I love being here. But how long can I last? I am very sorry for what I have done but cannot blame nobody but me.

Please God, help me through what I am going through. Lord, thank you for being here at Genesis House now.
Love,
Dolores.

5th December, 1984.

The house has been full for the last two weeks. There is Toby, who says she is 30 and looks 40, is extroverted, active and organises the other girls with great vigor and energy. Yet, she was crying today and wouldn't tell anyone the reason why.

Myrna, black and full of fear and resentment because of her color and weight, carryies with her a great load of insecurity and fear. Dolores, ready to relapse any moment, but torn by the comaraderie of the house and the deep need to belong.

Brenda, Lee and Kim, were here for a short visit.
Oh Lord, help us to know how we can nourish....

THE CHILDREN

Suddenly, our house is full
and we are empty and afraid.

Tania and her two baby boys,
beyond help, almost,
too damaged - too frightened
to ever be whole again,
too young, too hurt...

They huddled in corners,
against their mother's screams,
as her pimp raped and beat
and ravaged her.

The elder child
gathered all his seven years
and in desperate blind fury
attacked the raping pimp
with his red plastic truck.

Then, snarling in fury,
the pimp turned and
crashing his fist into
the child's face flung
him far across the room.

Lord, how can we nourish
such diminishment?
How can we tend such shoots
so bruised and ripped at the roots?

Ah, let me sleep rather than
know and see such fear and such pain -
so small and so inadequate
before this grief and deep suffering.

I don't know where to look,
but there, there, in my own
small sobbing kitchen, there it is,
all of it, around the table
and the empty coffee pot.

The children sitting
resentful, silent, hating.
I did not know,
that such pain
and such fear existed
in the hearts of babies.

5th December, 1984.

Lisa, who is eighteen, was brought in tonight by the police. A pimp
had brought her from Detroit to work the streets of Chicago. She tried
to escape and hid in launderettes and restaurants. After two weeks, she
was picked up by the police. That was her offer of freedom. We
talked to her, and she wants to go home. Tomorrow, we'll put her on a
train - older, wiser, aware of evil. But, what is home to her? She has
the same background as most of the other girls: broken family, incest,
alcoholism etc. They struggle against so many monsters, these little
children, and most of us do not even know.

Dolores: 6th December, 1984

Nineteen days till Christmas and I have not did anything. I have not
bought any presents yet. I really don't have any money except a few
dollars in the bank. I been doing O.K. I'm trying to gain them to trust
me. But maybe it is too early. There are times I feel a little jealous
with the girls here. I don't want to, and I'm trying my best also. You
never know, tomorrow may bring flowers, or maybe snow, for I may be
flowing with laughter.

Dolores: 7th December, 1984

Edwina,

For some reason I owe you an apology. I am sorry Edwina. I need help. I don't want a treatment program. But I know I need A.A. I am asking for some kind of support, "Yes" I know I have all the support. But what I need, help. Dolores.

7th December, 1984. Yorkville.

NIGHT

In the hermitage,
I find myself,
awed by blessings.
Outside, it is cold and crisp,
with a thin sheet of snow
half hiding the leaves.
The moon has risen high and white,
proud in the black sky,
amongst the stars.
The trees are stark and still,
casting shadows tall and twisted.
It is late, but I want to watch
the night light up,
beneath the pure moon.
It is late, but I want to see
the joy of light
in the darkness.
It is late, but I want to feel
its gentle power,
revealing, disclosing, transforming.
All of it is
breathing a great silence,
soothing to the soul.
I breathe deeply of the night's
incredible beauty,

and feel that I, too, am filled
with light and loveliness -
awed by blessings.

8th December, 1984. Chicago.

NAKEDNESS

There is something so real and earthy
about the woman prostitute.
She has nothing to hide,
nothing to cover up -
she has revealed all to lesser beings,
driven by lust or power.
So she parades herself, defiant
and aloof - nothing to hide,
nothing to treasure for herself.
She knows herself
and, alone in the darkness,
weeps for herself and
her own public nakedness.

GOD SLIPPED IN

God slipped into the brothel
when no one was looking
and sat amongst the ladies who
were drinking coffee and smoking reefers.
The jokes were loud and raucous,
the language harsh and strong,
until Debbie broke down and cried,
because a client refused to take her,
and threw her out with a curse,
useless, even for sex.
Than a hand reached out and held her.
A voice murmured, "We love you",

and in the silence, between the sobs,
I knew that God had slipped in,
sitting amongst the ladies,
in silent and painful compassion.

10th December, 1984

Dolores is back on the streets, drinking and already regretting it - how many times? Her good intentions last a few days and then - but it is so traumatic for all of us. We are getting firmer, more sure of our firmness - and reluctant to play the game. A little wiser - but the price we have paid for these long, painful lessons, has been high.

12th December, 1984

Dolores, back from the streets. She is very sick and is here under strict rules which she will surely break.

Dolores: 1st January, 1985

A new beginning.
I am also sober again today. Two weeks so far. I have to make it this time. It is my only chance. If I don't make it this time I will not ever make it.

                    Dolores.

5th January, 1985

Dolores began drinking again, just before I left for vacation in Florida. I want to pray that God will bend down and pick her up forever - that all this will soon be over for her and for me. Florida, surprisingly, is grey, cold and blustery. But perhaps that is the mood that most suits just now. What would I do with a brilliant sun and a clear, china blue sky? Ah, these days, they would laugh at me! Better an angry sky, and free, wild wind, so that together we can leap and toss about, grateful

for the sheer naked abandonment, gasping at the wild release of a
weary, long lived pain.

9th January, 1985

I am at a beautiful condo, near the beach. I am soaking it up - half
delighted in and half defiant of such wealth and leisure. There are
such extremes - the awful poverty and cringing misery of the streets -
and this - the palms, the pool, and thick-carpeted condo, fully equipped
with every device. God must tremble at the injustice, and weep for
those who can never enter or imagine such a place. And I live in the
two - longing for beauty and a little balance, dreaming of palm trees
and pools on the raped and ravaged streets.

20th January, 1985. Chicago.

THE SHELTER

The overnight shelter -
filled with hacking coughs,
and the pungent smell of
weary unwashed bodies, huddled
beneath three layers of
assorted second-hand clothing.
Plastic bags of pathetic possessions
(rescued from past buried
in painless oblivion)
are clutched jealously,
and tenderly patted
and shaped into pillows.
They sleep fully clothed,
these casualties of
our greed and ambition.
They sleep in great-coats
and heavy boots,
still dripping wet snow
onto the concrete floor.

They seethe with unspoken anger,
too bitter and violent
to find voice,
except in an occasional
fiery outburst of protest
sparked by a stolen cookie
or no cigarettes.
Reduced to survival,
fighting for the cookie,
or a cigarette,
whilst the world sleeps on -
safe and unaware.

21st January, 1985

The streets - on a cold night - women, wretched, lonely. Crystal, seething with anger and violence refused to leave the day shelter at locking-up time. I had to call in three guys from the streets to help. Lela, hysterical, called the police. It was hard to send them all out into the cold - hard to say, "It's time ladies...." Time again to move on - to no place of their own. It makes me feel very lonely. How does it feel in the morning when you wake up and it doesn't matter to anyone else?

29th January, 1985.

I spent the morning cooking beef stew for 200 street folks for evening dinner. This was the meal to follow the funeral services for Josie - the woman who froze to death in a dumpster behind McDonald's on New Year's Day. I gave the eulogy at the service. There were quite a lot of street people there and the event got T.V. coverage. Well, Josie's death provided the people with a fine dinner. Sad and ironic event. There are too many losers. I spent the rest of the evening at the women's drop-in center and ended my long day at the overnight shelter.

I surprise myself. I didn't know I could be so angry. I am full to capacity. Where is the dignity we owed Josie? How can the violence of her death touch me and anger me into more action? It is no good to claim that God loves her and she is now at rest. How can we be at rest? Aren't we responsible for her - her life and her death?

I am constantly looking for the balance in my life. If I allow all the violence and the pain to swallow me up, I'd be useless. I would become paralyzed at the magnitude of it. Of course, I can't shut it out, yet there has to be a part of me that does not sink beneath the anger and pain. It is this tiny part that can love, to wholeness, my suffering and beautiful brothers and sisters. It is the untouched part of me, which is perhaps the seed of God that is deep in all of us, that allows me to hope in the transformation of our world.

30th January, 1985.

Judy and I picked Dolores up from the streets - very ill, yellow and incoherent and smelling bad. We bathed her and drove her to hospital. I stayed with her all night. I have never seen her so bad. It was a hard night. She is so sick, I was afraid.

1st February, 1985

Dolores is very sick - in intensive care. God will have to stretch this miracle.

2nd February, 1985

Dolores was very critical last night and is still fighting. I am in hospital with her now, just waiting, watching. It is an awful time. Everything is hanging between life and death - it drains all energy and vitality. I have never seen her so bad. We pray.

THE HEALING

She lay heavy and hot on the hospital bed
her young skin puffed and yellow,
bruised with needles and careless cuts.
She breathed, rasping and shallow,
in a weary, mighty effort,
to snatch precious air and fleeing life.
A dozen tubes and bottles
thrust into the weary body,
fought with her for life,
her precious, precious life.

I turned to a saddened God
and pleaded,
"One more chance,
don't let her go, don't let her die
with needles and bottles and tubes"

I held her hand,
swollen and hot,
and with the force of a life of hope,
I thrust my faith,
alive and charged
into the sick and dying body.
I saw her jerk,
and then with a deep
weary sigh,
she fell back upon the pillow
into sleep, blessed sleep.
And I knew with a great certainty
that the God of life,
all compassion,
had, in that bright moment
bent down and kissed
her living child.

10th February, 1985. Yorkville.

GOD OF CREATION

God of the forest
I hear you whispering
high in the branches
of the fine, thick oaks.

God of the heavens
I see you gazing
thro' the silver streaked sunset
stretched over the land.

God of the earth
I feel your life-thrust
in the tender young crocus
bursting thro' the soil.

God of the waters
I taste your gentle grace
in the pure cooling stream
rushing by the rocks.

God of all that is,
I embrace your beating heart
in soil and sky and foliage
and the very air we breathe.

11th February, 1985. Yorkville.

The silence today calls forth a sadness in me. Is it the thousand memories locked away so deep, they can only be sensed? Does silence, utter silence touch deep inside me, what nothing else can touch? What wild young dream would rise up in all its nakedness from such silence? Beautiful and painful, fulfilling and tragic, I experience this silence and its mysterious possibilities. Aloneness of this quality is rare. I sense it and welcome it but I can never fully or clearly comprehend or enter into it. I don't think I can do much more than sense it, touch it, brush it perhaps. It doesn't go anywhere or produce anything - it's a kind of suspended quality awareness. Yes, that's about the nearest description I can come up with. It must be charged with God. That's where the sense of awe and mystery come from. Is it that I'm sitting down with God then? This, then is prayer in its deepest form, and I didn't even recognise it. Or, did I?

Dolores: 13th February, 1985

Feeling well enough to write.

I am in University of Illinois Hospital. I came so close to die. I'm getting better. Had about ten tests since I been here. I been here two weeks today. I have been having a lot of support since I been here from Genesis. I been having visitors every day here. I been a little depressed since I been here. Not really depress but lonely. Since I been here this last week I been thinking I'm very scared to take a drink again. I don't want to drink anymore. It might sound like a re-run but in my heart it does not.

The doctors are good here. I'm happy that I know there is someone, some people that care and I have a home to go to, when I leave hospital. It has been a miracle that I am still alive. Genesis is the best thing that ever happened to me and I love it.

Dolores: 16th February, 1985

Today has been a strange, cold, slow day. But Ted visited me and put a shiny star in my eye. Last night I slept very early like 6.30. Slept my depression away. I'm trying to get in a good mood (good spirit). I will. I will think of all the good things I still have in my life.

18th February, 1985.

Ted and I brought Dolores home from the hospital tonight. She is still very sick and weak. I feel moved by a very deep compassion and tenderness for her - it is so hard to see her dying.

Dolores: 20th February, 1985

I been out of hospital since Monday. I feel a little weak. But gradually each day I feel a little better. Each day I'm getting plenty of rest eating good (the right) foods. I now at Genesis. All the community been so good to me. I also take medicine. Change my leg bandage four times a day. So I have many blessings to thank for. I plan to live here as long as it takes me to get myself together. I hope even longer because I cannot take being in this world alone. Not for a long time because I'm scared. Scared of every-thing and everyone.

Dolores.

2nd March, 1985

A long time since I wrote - no special reason, except an indication that I need to give myself a little more time just for me.

Dolores is still very weak and yellow. She will never get well.

GOD RAN AWAY

God ran away
when we imprisoned her
and put her in a box
named Church.
God would have none
of our labels and
our limitations
and she said,
"I will escape and plant myself
in a simpler, poorer soil
where those who see, will see,
and those who hear, will hear.
I will become a God - believable,

because I am free,
and go where I will.
My goodness will be found
in my freedom and
that freedom I offer to all -
regardless of color, sex or status,
regardless of power or money.
Ah, I am God
because I am free
and all those who would be free
will find me,
roaming, wandering, singing.
Come, walk with me -
come, dance with me!
I created you to sing - to dance -
to love....."

If you cannot sing,
nor dance, nor love,
because they put you
also in a box,
know that your God broke free
and ran away.
So, send your spirit
then, to dance with Her.
Dance, sing with the God
whom they cannot tame nor chain.
Dance within, though they chain
your very guts
to the great stone walls....
Dance, beloved,
Ah, Dance!

Dolores: 8th March, 1985

So far so good. I'm happy but there are times when I feel ecky.

Sick. I'm restless at night. I don't sleep all through the night. I straightened all my belongings and miscellaneous, so now I'm down to

one box and one laundry basket. The only thing I have that's working right is my heart. I have a heart of love. Thank you Lord for all my blessings and especially for being alive today.
           Dolores.

13th March, 1985

A lot of chaos!

The police brought Aicha - a Moroccan girl, lured to this country under false pretenses of marriage all the way from Morocco by a pimp and pressed into prostitution - another casualty. She weeps in humiliation and bewilderment.

15th March, 1985. Yorkville.

JUST A LITTLE DIFFERENCE

Ah - a resting place, perhaps
where we come to understand
it is not required of us
to wrestle constantly and passionately
with our God -
nor pursue relentlessly
all God's decrees as we understand them,
but only that we listen and wonder
and hope and pray,
that we might, perhaps,
make just a little difference,
one quiet grey day.

15th April, 1985

Jesus ended up with nothing, because he was faithful. He refused to be God. Refused to be their God. Jesus started, after time in the desert, an energetic, passionate proclamation of the Kingdom ministry, healing, liberating, calling forth. All around him there was lots of energy and passion, until he quit the miracles and started talking about suffering and death and Jerusalem. They couldn't understand! They were disappointed! They all left! Jesus lost everything - nothing left. I have to go too.

It's all God's business.

Dolores: 18th March, 1985

It has been a very long time since I have written. I just have not been in the mood I guess, but these days been good for me. A lot of support, loving and caring and well taking care of me and I am happy. There are times when I feel still weak but today I can say I am a lot stronger. I have not been out lately. Thought came through me that I might be a little scared but eventually I will get over it.
                    Dolores.

20th April, 1985 Yorkville.

DEATH OF THE HERMITAGE

Spring - everything thrusting, bursting,
and oh - the utter delight I feel,
to sit among the daffodils and the still
unopened tulips
growing in bright clusters around the hermitage.

I remember planting them years ago.
They grow strong and tall as the hermitage
rusts and sags,
dignified but dying.
The roof leaks, the wood warps,
and great cracks appear on the outside walls.
My hermitage, splendid, sacred place,

home of tiny mice, spiders and gods.
My hermitage is dying,
but the daffodils dance around its death
as I sit and watch it in lonely,
loving mourning.

When it crumbles and dies,
what will die in me?

Dolores: 20th April, 1985

Today is a special day. Mark's birthday. 66 yrs. old. Edwina and Stella and I went to Yorkville for the day. 3 months I been sober.

I am happy.

Very well also.

Dolores: 21st April, 1985

Was a very good and I say Hot (warm) day. Had a lazy morning (exhausted from Yorkville). We had a barbeque today. Just the three of us, Judy, Edwina and me.

Steak! Salad and artichokes, ice tea and then went to the theater. What a treat (Passage to India)....and ice cream cones.
        Dolores.

29th April, 1985

THE WOMEN'S SHELTER

The narrow wooden stairs are scuffed and broken,
a sharp stale smell hangs in the air, and hovers
over the threadbare carpet.

The pathetic stairwell leads to a long narrow room,
simple and shabby, filled with an assortment
of rejected furniture.

But, ah, the real rejects slump in the broken windows,
and sprawl, uncaring and unconscious, across the couches,
covered with blankets, to hide the bursting padding and
protruding springs.

The street ladies - here they flee from the threat
and nakedness of the cold streets;
here they hide, scrunched up in corners, drinking
donated coffee and pleading for cigarettes.

The ladies, blanketed humps, bury their weary
bodies deep in the sweaty mattresses, and dream,
perhaps of love, and perfume, and clear blue skies,
remembering with cruel clarity, days past,
when they knew laughter, hope and a bed
they called their own.

But now they awake to angry curses, the smell of
unwashed bodies and the terrifying reality of
what they are. No hope, no future here.
The only dream is Tuesday's bingo, when everyone
gets a prize - the highlight of the week.

What tragedy struck you Margaret, that now,
in your prime, you choose to curl and die in
this dismal place?
What sorrow paralysed you, Lee, that your
once lovely eyes now are veiled in an awful
deadness - impenetrable?

What killed your spirit, Judy, that now you
drag so hopelessly your listless, still strong
body around these filthy streets?

Ah, ladies of the street, casualties of lust

and violence and love-lessness!
May your dingy darkened lives cast a shadow
over the candles of our altars.
May your lonely tears and solitude,
break with passion into our cosy suburban homes.
May your silent dying be somehow, somewhere -
not forgotten.

Dolores: 9th May, 1985.

My birthday. I'm 30 today. What a beautiful day. A Rememberance I will never forget. Got many presents. The food was good. Most of all, my friends. I wanted to cry. I think I did. 30 years. What an age! Thank you Lord for letting me see this day alive and HAPPY.

Dolores: 16th May, 1985.

I'm hurting in my stomach. I'm really bad for not telling anybody. I see a little blood in my urine. I will call the doctor in the morning. I'm worried that I will get put back in the hosp. again. I don't want to see a hospital bed again.
                                        Dolores.

17th May, 1985

Full house - Dolores, Alma, Sandy, Lori and Lee, David from Tuscon (also visiting us), bought us all extravagent ice cream - it was like bringing candies for the children. We all loved it, and were filled with a precious sense of innocence and joy.

These women, so hurt and violated and bruised: Lee - the hardened hooker; Sandy - the gang basher; Lori - the prostitute; Dolores - the alcoholic; Alma - the street woman.....just enjoying ice cream and giggling, like the kids they never were. Lee and Sandy wanted to pray, so the three of us went downstairs into the basement chapel. They talked freely and seriously about God in their lives - "God don't do no shit", said Lee vehemently. "God is the only one who don't do no shit, I talk to God - God talks to me, I can hear him. Sometimes when me and Vernon is sitting watching T.V., and I go all quiet, and Vernon says "What's up?". I say, "I'm listening to God".   I know God is right with me when I'm out on the streeets, or I wouldn't be alive today. I don't need a book or a cathedral. I just need God." Sandy says she prays every night on her knees - "Can't pray unless I'm kneeling", she says, "I gotta kneel to God."

These women are sincere, without guile or hypocrisy - they take God without judgement or gratification. Their faith is enormous. They are a grace for me.

18th May, 1985

Dolores is not at all well. She is swollen and beginning to bleed. I am very afraid. I feel the cold fear creeping around me again. She is still a joy to me. I feel like a mother.

> While You Die
> Let me hold your hand
> while you die.
> Let me smile with you
> while you die.
> Let me walk with you
> while you die.
> Let me hold and kiss you
> while you die.
> Ah - let me die a little with you
> so that all might learn to love.

"Yes, I am making a road in the wilderness, paths in the wild."
(Is. 43: 19)

Dolores: 19th May, 1985

Slept most of the day. Had diarreah, headache and back pains. I'm sick throwing up. Edwina is in Yorkville. There is a party tomorrow for her birthday. I don't want to be sick on Edwina's birthday party, but I will do my best.

27th May, 1985

Genesis House is full - lots of action and a little healing. Jo, who we thought was a woman, but after three days, discovered s/he was a man, is staying with us in the basement. We may be able to do a little for him/her....the prostitutes have less problems accepting transexuals than we Christians do.

We also have Michelle, a sixteen-year-old runaway. It really is a family, and a handful! I'm possibly too soft with them, but there is mutual respect. There are too many late nights for me! I am tired today.

2nd June, 1985

THE MASSACRE OF FORESTS

The wind told the trees of the massacre of their
brothers, deep down in the far south of the land.
The wind saw it, and screeched and cried, driving
herself northward with the tale of destruction
howling in her billows.

And the trees of the north shook and rocked in
the embrace of the wind;
Heavens and roots trembled at the senseless acts of human greed.
The wind gentled, whispered away, leaving the trees standing stark,
stretched out, all-knowing,
grieving against the reddened sky.

Did anyone cry for you before, forest?
Forgive us, Mother, for raping you.

5th June, 1985. Chicago.

It was an interesting day - full of contrasting events. The morning I
spent at a workshop on Incest. Then I had lunch at the brothel with
May. The girls, as always were waiting for dates. Then I met an
anxious young salesman who talked about his daughter, and then,
commented how good Betty had been in the bedroom. After that, I
went to the Pastoral Center to meet a band of Bishops at a hearing for
the first draft of the Mission Pastoral.

Incest - Brothel - Bishops - How fitting!!

6th June, 1985.

FLIGHT

By the lake at Loyola, I have fled like a fugitive
from days filled with people, action, events!
From alcoholics and hookers, who for all their
shining beauty and openness, can drain every ounce
of energy and patience from me.

I can feel the weariness and irritation crawling
through me and I know I must leave and be alone
and hear the water rising, falling, dancing on the beach.
Ah - I feel the warm breeze, as it were, gently
brushing away my fatigue, and soothing just a little,
my frayed sense of self.

There are tiny sails on the horizon and I carry
myself to them over the tossing water, setting
loose my spirit to leap and play in sea and sky,

        run free and wild - gathering from the elements
    energy and life to seep thro' me, and set me walking
            with new and gentler wisdom
        Yes gentler, much gentler wisdom.

7th June, 1985

Sometimes (often), this house is like a circus. There is always something happening and many evenings we go from one "crisis" to another. Jo, the young transexual, spaced out, not getting on with what she should be about - coming home late, drifting.

Sandy with her intolerance and youthfulness - all bright and smart and "with it" cool.

Lori - clinging to Roy who treats her like shit and obviously has no time for her, unable to get her life together because of her obsessive dependency on him. There are constant fights which get her so upset. She could miscarry.

Dolores - thank God she's stable.

Long late nights full of these women's terrors and loneliness.

12th June, 1985

I can't remember when I last sat alone downstairs in Genesis House in the evening with music playing. Rare moments! Dolores, Sandy, Lori and Jo, all in bed by 11.00 p.m!

Later. It was ten minutes of complete quietness and stillness - peace - quality. Very good. We are learning to take a little space.

Dolores: 14th June, 1985

Today I feel very proud of myself. I registered in school at College, "Vocabulary in Development"! I went walking without any attempt to drink. So I was out most of the afternoon.

Dolores: 15th June, 1985

I started school today. It went very good. Judy took me out for Chinese dinner. I surprise Edwina and sat in her car! She didn't know I was there. So my whole day was fun and busy. I feel so happy I can cry!

Dolores: 17th June, 1985

Went out for a little while. Cooked supper in the evening. I went walking around. I feel more active now more than I even done in a long time. I think I have Edwina and Judy's trust.

Dolores.

21st June, 1985

Dolores left three days ago - she was doing so well. We tried - hoped. I don't dare think how much longer she will survive. There is nothing I can do, should do except wait. Wait. I have a little quiet time now....it is 9.00 p.m. All the women are out. I will have an hour I think. It is so rare to find the house empty. I can listen to music and sit by the lamp. I am aware of a fearful sadness in the pit of my stomach.

My mind is somewhat frayed, distracted because of my concern for Dolores - but I have to live through this again. God knows I have done it often enough.

Oh, I am so thankful for these quiet moments. Soothing like water flowing over dry rocks.

22nd June, 1985 - Yorkville.

DOLORES

No news of Dolores.
I walk thro' the forest
hear the birds sing,
see the profusion of leaves
and wild flowers,
and pray that, somehow, soon
her misery will be over,
and she will hear the birds sing
and see the profusion of leaves
and wild flowers.
Soon, she and I,
will both be free,
when God, in her great compassion
stoops to gently gather her
in her arms.

It is enough - It is enough!

23rd June, 1985. Chicago.

I found Dolores drunk on the sidewalk.   Sicker, lower than ever.
Awful destruction. Crushing of the blossom. I am dazed with sadness.
It is time for God to gather her up. I have loved her so much.

24th June, 1985

I called Fr. Jim Doyle s.j., today, to make sure he would be at my talk
on street ministy tonight at the University. But, I was told he died on
Saturday. Another death! He gave birth to my street ministry - or at
least, was the midwife. He supported and encouraged me during that
long period of retreat and discernment when I struggled so hard with
this call to minister on the streets. I loved and honored him. His death,
his loss leaves me numb.

25th June, 1985

I spent the morning with May and patiently listened to her violence. Then I went to see Jim laid out in the chapel of the Jesuit Residence, at Loyola University. I don't think I have ever shared so much at such a deep level with anyone else. He shared my dream, but above all, he believed in it and trusted it, so I was able to. I don't think I could have done it without him. Afterwards I sat and watched the waters of Lake Michigan.

26th June, 1985

WILL YOU?

When I'm too tired to look at you,
and my eyes are heavy and drowsy,
will you, Lord, look instead at me?

When my mind is too full to think of you,
and thoughts and memories absorb me,
will you, Lord, think instead of me?

When I'm too busy to listen to you,
and my day is packed with demands and noise,
will you, Lord, listen instead to me?

When I'm too blind to see your faint,
thin path and stumble along in haste,
will you, Lord, walk ahead of me?

Ah, will you, Lord, gather me up
like a mother her chick,
and love me, through all
with a joyous passion?

30th June, 1985

Dolores came home swollen and very frightened. She cried in bed and whispered, "I won't die tonight, will I?" It makes me afraid too. I am glad she is home. This has to be the last time she comes home. I am very tired today.

1st July, 1985

It was not the last time. Dolores left again today.

Dolores: 6th July, 1985

Oh well, I did it again. I went out on another drunk and got caught. What makes it bad - Judy and Maria picked me off the street, on the street bench. I'm detoxing here in Yorkville. If I can make it through just three days I will feel much better. I have not written in such a long time. I thought I have forgot. I will stop for now because my hands are shaking too much right now.

Dolores.

7th July, 1985. Yorkville - The Hermitage

The only sound is that of birds vying with each other to sing the most harmonious and rich evening song, closing the day, preluding night's gentle silence. Ah - there cannot anywhere be a more beautiful, soothing sound than this cascade of wild and dizzy music, trembling through the forest, declaring God's faithfulness. Only when the fool is born can the miracles occur, when intellect gives way to simplicity, and reason to joy.

8th July, 1985

This is my last day in the hermitage before the VMM family moves out of Yorkville at the end of next month. We have to move because the religious society which owns the property is selling. And we, as laity, will be without a home again. How hard it is for lay people who are called to ministry to be included in this status-hierarchical oriented church! My hermitage will be lost also.

I expected it to be painful, full of nostalgia, but so far it has been a gentle experience. I am saying goodbye to trees and birds, paths and creek, to this magnificent clearing in the forest. But as I say my good-byes I know that I have experienced life fully here and it is time to return the gift, with gratitude to God.

I GIVE BACK TO YOU

I give back to you, Creator God,
this lovely place,
this sacred corner,
the song of these birds,
in the evening and early morning.
I return to you,
the silence of the woods and
the blackness of the deep night.
I return to you
the fresh wild flowers
peering from leafy undergrowth and
the joyous butterflies
flitting over the water.

But I myself will keep,
Creator God,
the memory of awed and
wondrous moments held spellbound
amongst the beauty of this place.
I myself will keep

the vision of morning sunlight
leaping through the trees,
the shining mystery of
the spider's web spun
across my path.

Ah, I myself will keep
the quick tears and
running laughter,
the awed awareness
which strung my soul
to this splendid,
splendid place.

Spirit of the trees,
you shared with me
your strength and rootedness,
your brave solidity
against the elements.

Spirit of the earth
you shared with me
your rich moist warmth,
your nurturing
embracing presence.

Spirit of the grasses,
you shared with me
your rhythmic gentleness,
your gay and joyous dances.

Spirit of the wild,
wild flower,
you shared with me
your delicate wholesomeness,
your rich rare perfume
born only for a moment
when the falling sun
threw its last light

over the dusked earth.

Spirit of all creation,
you unleashed in me
just a little,
just a little of
God's great loveliness.

I need to be in touch with the earth if I am to continue experiencing my own sense of one-ness with it. Intimacy with the earth leads to an intimacy with my own unique createdness and a sense of belonging to all of creation. When I am out of touch with earth, I am dis-connected from part of my soul.

"Do not hold on to the gifts I give to you,
the beauty I reveal to you.
I am everywhere.
You will find my beauty everywhere -
new and fresh, always delighting.
The birds will sing a different song, that's all.
The earth will still smell moist and fresh,
its spring will be new, that's all.
I, the God of these woods,
am also the God of all the earth."

Thank you, living God, for all the joys and sorrows and wonders of having this hermitage in the forest. Thank you for this finest gift of all - the cup that ran over. Ah - thank you, living God, for this sacred dwelling place. Let me take with me its soul and spirit and let its form return to the womb of the earth. Thank you, Great Forest, for leading me to God's City.

Dolores: 10th July, 1985

I'm home now at Genesis House. Still a little nervous. I went to A.A. - feeling better about myself. Scared but this is what I must do. It feels good to be in my own room and sleeping in my bed. Thank you, Lord, for this.

Dolores: 11th July, 1985

I call this my First Day. Because I made some commitments with my counsellor, Jack. I feel much better since I seen and talked to Jack. He is the best counsellor I have ever had. He understands.

Anyways, my day was good. I felt myself getting bored so I did something in the house. I did not think of a drink. I was happy and felt good about myself today. I'm grateful to be sober today. Still a little shaky but it all will pass very soon.

It went very well today with my meeting with Jack. I'm so glad that we had our talk. I see him twice a week. I agreed to go to three meetings a week. So I'm happy I am sober today.

Dolores: 12th July, 1985

My day was good. Went to the clinic. My Doctor was upset because I told her that I was drinking for which I don't blame her. I was alone part of the afternoon. I did think of sneaking out and getting a drink. But I did not.

Dolores: 17th July, 1985

What a day. But I made it through. I was alone all day till 7.00 p.m. o'clock. I had to hurry to a meeting. I was so scared. I have to be careful now. Because I can feel myself that I's going to take that first drink. I feel no support at all. I tried to call Jack. No answer. I have to try to pull myself together. What's wrong? I know I am an alcoholic and it is cunning. I have no more control, but I have to, if not it will take the best of me and I won't let it. It's like a war going on. I feel I'm the only person against this Big War. I don't know what I'm doing wrong. I'm doing everything to keep Dolores sober. But how much can Dolores take?

Dolores: 21st July, 1985

It's been a good day. Went to church in Wayne, Ill. Edwina did two homilies there. The people were so different, specially their backgrounds. They don't know anything about the homeless or alcoholics. One lady, when I told her I was an alcoholic, she looked at me like I was shit. Made me feel hurt but I said to myself afterwards, "Screw her."

Dolores: 24th July, 1985

I have not written in a week. Very busy since I have been writing in another journal for Jack. I ignored my own journal. But I'm happy and in good spirits. I see Jack tomorrow. I'm starting to like myself again. Not love quite yet. Thank you Lord, for this day - that I lived another day. Very grateful for this house.

Dolores: 26th July, 1985

What a wonderful day I had. Went on a boat (special boat) on the lake for the day with Edwina, Gypsy and some friends. Funny when I was on the boat I seemed I left all my problems on shore for them four and a half hours. What a relief it was.

Dolores.

9th August, 1985. Chicago.

Dolores left again and is on the streets drinking. Lately I am always a little numb when this happens. I experience a gut level sadness and foreboding, but I feel I am in control of it rather than the other way around. I can, for instance, continue this day as normal, not allowing Dolores' behavior to wreak disaster on myself. I am calm, sad, older. I wonder when it will all be over and both of us can rest.

Sandy had to run away to avoid being put back into an official shelter. She has gone from shelter to shelter since the age of ten, when she finally convinced the courts her mother abused her physically. Her body is still witness to the cigarette burns and her mind still bears the scars of lovelessness. Oh, how cruel and unbending the law and society can be! She was fine with us, but we are not licensed and cannot house minors. she has had enough of institutions for which she is a name and number in a file. Bureaucracy has no tenderness or compassion.

Sandy needs a mother, a family so she can be a child with potential for growth. I feel the problems and pains of Genesis House and the women we care for creeping up on me like the sea on the beach. Society does not do enough for its casualties - Genesis House is a haven, but when they leave it, the world is too cruel and closed to receive them and know how to love them.

Dolores is drunk on the streets, Sandy is on the run from society and red tape, and Lori lost her job. And all we can do is watch and hurt.

20th September, 1985.

I received a letter from Mezzie in Jail. Mezzie works the streets and is an addict. She was abandoned as an infant, brought up in an orphanage and abused by two foster families at ages eight and eleven. Not surprisingly, she hit the streets as a twelve-year-old runaway and has spent the last twenty six years or so trying to survive the only way she knew. She has been in and out of jail countless times but underneath all the toughness, hostility and anger, Mezzie is a beautiful, intelligent and deeply wounded woman who never stood a chance - until she came to Genesis House and made a new start in life. But she was too badly bruised to succeed this time. The police picked her up on old warrants and back she is behind bars:

"Dear Edwina,

Here I am, sitting in familiar surroundings....well, maybe when I get out the world will have changed. But, maybe, I'm here because the God you tell me about believes in me - maybe this God is saying, "I don't make no junk. Mezzie's rusty, has a few holes and she needs a lot of work, so I'll send her to the shop. I'll lead her to heal herself."

I can't afford to feel comfortable, Edwina. For me that's accepting my dope mentality. I need to look at my life and see where I'm all screwed up. But I also need to let the positive things I've done soak in and become me. If I do this I won't keep thinking of myself as worthless and negative. I'll see me as you do.

You believed in me and I tried. Someday, I'll believe in me too. I'd hate to die here in jail or die face down in some cooker of dope. But if I do, remember that I knew you loved me.

When you're young, you trust in your parents. I had none. I trusted in the dope man and he failed me and left his legacy in my blood. My life has reinforced my disbelief in me. Edwina, please don't let my failure stop your work. Remember I was 38 before I met you. Take care of our dreams to fight for women like me. Don't give up hope.

When you go out to give talks, carry our message to the people you speak to. Tell them that we are all God's children, and that nobody was born into this world trying to be negative. Tell them we all came with great expectations that our lives would be happy and fruitful. So if they can't help us to recover, and find happiness in life, ask them not to hurt us.

Love,

    Mezzie."

How long will it be before we stop hurting those already so badly wounded and abused?

PART VI: A NEW CREATION

4th October, 1985

Dolores died in a transient hotel early yesterday morning - or
it may have been late on the 2nd. It is all over.
Dear one, rose on the Broadway. I came too late for you,
Dolores. Peace. Rest, loved one. It is all over now.
No more running, no more anguish. No more pain. No more joy with
you, special beautiful lady.

7th October, 1985

Today we had Dolores' funeral service. It was a beautiful tribute to
her. Almost a hundred people, both street people and suburbanites
came - priests, pimps, nuns, prostitutes, white, black, rich, poor - all
rubbing shoulders around my dead Dolores. These were people who
had met and had come to love Dolores.

We managed to contact her family, who came. Her mother, sisters and
brothers all came. Even her son, eight years old, and not sure who it
was who had died, came. They couldn't understand why Dolores was
so hurt. Many of the women have respectable families who do not
understand how the family sickness can be lived out by one of its
members.

A woman journalist came from New York, not to write a story, but to
say goodbye to Dolores, who she had come to love when doing an
article a year ago. Street people, some carrying their plastic bags full
of garbage, came one by one to see, for the last time, the Teddy Bear
they knew. Mark, Eskimo Joe, the women of Genesis House, Su,
Maria, Judy, the VMM community and I came to proclaim to the world
that this Rose of the Broadway will live on in our hearts.

"Dolores, dear one, you were loved. You were beautiful!
It was a long, painful day. It is too soon for me to grieve.
Ah - for all the anguish, I will miss you. It will never be quite the
same."

8th October, 1985.

I am alone. I don't know how I feel. I tip-toe around in fragility. After all these years - I wish I had been with her at her death. But she knows I was with her so often, so long. She knows now how much I loved and anguished for her.

10th October, 1985

DISCIPLE OF JESUS

Disciple of Jesus, weary and silent,
aware, in the darkness of challenges
failed and longings unfilled,
remembering the passion that sent you forth,
young and bright, and fired with hope.

Disciple of Jesus, weary and silent,
world unchanged, its darkness still deep,
dreams dispelled and visions blurred,
How is it now with you?

Trailing behind me the sparkle and fire
of early passion,
bruised and tender from love's long thrust.
Now is the finest, greatest moment
and now the ultimate death.

For I, Disciple of Jesus,
to stand before my God,
weary, silent, and all alone,
claiming only, "I was there"

14th October, 1985

I went walking on the beach, empty and beautiful, aware of God's presence and Dolores, smiling, encouraging....

I experienced peace and a quiet joy. I know deeply that I now have an angel in heaven. Now it is not I who am her guardian, but she who is mine. Her special care is for the VMM, and for Genesis House. We will receive many blessings. There will be a shower of roses from the woman whom I shall always think of as a rose growing on the Broadway.

15th October, 1985

Death is not the end, but the beginning of the rest of eternity. It is the final summary of our lives - the moment when we meet ourselves, face to face, with no masks to obscure our very selves.

I was too late to change her path into one of claiming life for herself. But now she knows life. Now she knows herself. And I have loved her, and she knew it. She died knowing herself loved and that is surely, surely the most precious thing I could have ever offered her. That was God's miracle.

26th October, 1985

I have not written lately. Instead I remember Dolores - full of joy and smiling. My experience of Dolores and my love for her will bear fruit for other women in this great and lonely city. There are many Teddy Bears. Many, many Dolores'. We have only just begun.

7th January, 1986.

I walked on the beach, completely deserted and all white and shining with frozen snow. The sun was bright, though the air was very cold. It was beautiful! I thought of Dolores and how she would have enjoyed walking by the lake she loved so well. In the frozen silence I smiled as I felt her presence, like a new creation - alive and free.

It is a new year.

The Volunteer Missionary Movement (VMM) was founded by Edwina Gateley in England in 1969. It has provided hundreds of missionaries for ministries in many countries. In 1981 Su Hood became the first director of the VMM–USA in Illinois, when Edwina lived in the hermitage in the forest next to the VMM community house. By January 1990, the VMM–USA had prepared and sent 70 North American members overseas to serve the peoples of Africa, Papua New Guinea and the West Indies.

Genesis House was founded in Chicago, Illinois in January 1984, and in its first six years has offered services and support to over 4000 women involved in a lifestyle of prostitution. Almost 400 women have left prostitution through the work of Genesis House. A number of women who have gone through programs at Genesis House now work as staff members and others serve as members of the Board of Directors.

Genesis House and the VMM are not-for-profit organizations, dependent for money on grants and donations and Edwina's speaking and writing. Four of Edwina's recent talks are available on audiocassette, wherever books and tapes are sold, or directly from the publisher. Edwina's first book, *Psalms of A Laywoman,* now in its sixth printing, is also available. If you would like to find out about her speaking schedule, or would like to engage her to speak to your group, or are able to donate to VMM or Genesis House, please contact the publisher:

Source Books, Box 794, Trabuco Canyon CA 92678 USA.

TALKS BY EDWINA GATELEY ON AUDIOCASSETTE

I Hear God Laughing (Source)
Giving Birth to God (Source)
Rediscovering and Claiming the Feminine Soul (Source)
Discipleship (St. Anthony Messenger Press)